Striking for Ford

Alan Dixon

Clink Street

Published by Clink Street Publishing 2021

Copyright © 2021

First edition.

ISBN:
978-1-913962-37-1 - paperback
978-1-913962-38-8 - ebook

Contents

Eavesdropping

I had been in my new job three hours, when I was told there was going to be an indefinite strike. 'For God's sake,' I said to myself, as I was ushered into the Personnel Manager's office at the sprawling car factory in Liverpool. Twenty personnel staff were crammed into a tar yellow, dingy office, listening intently to someone from Head Office in London on a tabletop speaker phone.

Eric Moore, the Personnel Manager shouted into the phone, 'We've just been joined by our new labour relations trainee Frank Thomas, it's his first day in the factory.'

'Welcome Frank,' laughed a cockney voice over the speaker, and I waved weakly as everyone turned to look at me.

'Unbloody believable, starting work the day of an indefinite pay strike, that's gotta be a first even for Liverpool. That's cheered me up that has. Eric, call me when the stewards have reported back to their members,' and still laughing, he rang off.

Eric stood and beckoned me to the front of the room.

'Frank, that guy leads the company pay negotiations with the blue-collar unions in London. Now, Jim's your mentor and he'll introduce you to everyone later, but as time is of the essence, can you write in the dark?'

'Write in the dark?' I said.

'Just get yourself a clipboard and go with Jim to the press shop canteen.' I noticed a wry grin on his face. The shop stewards' committee's meeting in the canteen to decide on recommending or rejecting today's pay offer. You and Jim are going to hide in the kitchen and take notes about what they say.'

'What, like spying on them?' I said.

'No, eavesdropping. Now, Jim will show you the ropes and by the way, welcome to industrial relations.'

The others sniggered as we left. Jim, the colleague assigned to lead my induction and I walked towards the factory floor. We passed the factory personnel offices, known apparently as the 'piggeries'. I was only just into the job and was beginning to wonder about my career choice, but then thought of a college friend who had also accepted a traineeship, only to be offered redundancy a month before she'd even started.

I had a new suit from a cheap high street chain store and felt out of sorts in a shirt and tie after three years at college but was determined to stick at a professional job. I needed the money and good jobs in the depressed British economy were like gold dust. I followed Jim deep into the car factory, assaulted on all sides by mechanical noise, insanely bright fluorescent strip lights, continuous spot-welding flashes and the sickly smell of cutting oil. Cars rolled slowly down the lines, swarmed over by an army of workers in boiler suits.

'Stay close,' said Jim in his strong scouse accent, as he unlocked the door to the canteen. He led me across to a second door next to a shuttered serving hatch, unlocked it and went in, pulling it shut on the latch. We were alone in a windowless kitchen, with barely enough light to see by.

'When the stewards come in, get your ear as close to the hatch as possible and write down everything they say, exactly mind.'

'Won't they check in here?' I whispered.

'They'll rattle the door, see it's locked and carry on. If they find us, they'll go apeshit.'

'Are we listening to see how many stewards vote to recommend the pay strike then?' I said.

'Nah. A strike is an absolute cert. Senior management just want to know if the stewards blame the company or the government's pay ceiling.'

I frowned and looked through the gloom at Jim's greasy blue suit, his curled-up lip and face that looked in the half-light like one of those gaunt underfed images from war photographs. He was about forty years old, with round shoulders and a lopsided grin. Is this me if I stay working here? I sat on the serving counter near to the shutter.

'Shush... they're here,' Jim said.

I jumped as someone rattled the kitchen door and could hear my heartbeat above the muffled voices assembling in the main canteen.

'Lads, even our union officials are saying the company is hiding behind the incomes policy to offer a piffling 5% across the board,' a tough sounding Glaswegian boomed out.

'As ye know, last year we got just 2% above the guideline and this year we want 20%.' A murmur of approval rippled round the room. Behind the shutter I lost my balance and rattled the shutter. There was silence from the stewards outside.

'Jack, check that door, I would nae put spying past the excuses for management we've got.'

We held our breath as the door handle rattled heavily.

'It's locked la, must be the wind or the canteen rats,' said Jack, whoever he was.

I could hear the muffled laughter from the stewards,

'Bloody hell,' I whispered.

The union convenor must have turned to face the other way as it was then only possible to hear fragments of speech.

I wrote down the few words I could hear, the pen shaking:

'Inflation's over 16% and we also wanna line workers' allowance... mass meeting Speke football ground between shifts as normal... show of hands will do...'

The meeting was winding down and the stewards were filing out. As I eased myself off the counter, the door handle rattled loudly again, followed by a shoulder charge against the door.

'Just leave it, you'll damage the door, knobhead,' said an unknown voice.

'There's some twat in there I swear,' it sounded like Jack.

We froze, waiting fifteen long minutes before Jim carefully unlocked the door. I could feel the sweat running down my back, my bri-nylon shirt would soon be sticky. Jim peeped around the door and immediately shut it again and said, 'They're still standing by the main door in the corridor, we'll use the rear fire escape, the bastards.'

We groped our way out towards the back of the kitchen preparation area, where Jim unlocked yet another door. I flinched at the bright factory lights but followed Jim carefully down a steel fire escape emerging somewhere inside the factory, completely unknown to me. We walked quickly back to the main offices.

'Close run thing that, nearly shat myself there,' Jim pronounced, sounding relieved as he went to brief Bill. I raised my eyebrows, acknowledging my gaffe with the shutter door then relaxed into my new chair, glad the incident was over.

I felt excited about my first ever office even though it was more like a large cubicle. I sat on a worn green swivel chair, spun round, and took in the small space. It was aluminium framed, with half-windowed partitions, a metal desk and a second chair for visitors. Five yards away from the corridor outside the office, was the entrance to the factory. As people came and went, I could hear the distant crashes of the jigs dropping car bodies into place and I became aware of an emerging migraine. I wasn't sure if it was due to the stress of the canteen eavesdropping or having to get up at seven o'clock that morning. I wasn't used to being awake before ten o'clock in my last year at college. I pompously decided to take my first ever work decision and wrote 'buy another suit' in my desk diary. I didn't want my only suit going greasy like Jim's.

A sharp knock on the glass separating the office from the one next door startled me. An Asian-looking girl about my own age peered over holding up two cups of Klix coffee. I nodded as she came round to the door.

'It's hot and wet.'

I took in the full smile and dark bob, noticing the smart black skirt and jacket with shoulder pads. I blinked; she was a sight for sore eyes in this dump.

'Hi. I'm Anita, I was due to do your factory tour now but it's off,' she said with an unusually posh Birmingham accent.

I vaguely recognised her from the meeting in the personnel office earlier.

'There's a mass meeting on the pay strike for blue collars starting soon,' she continued, 'so nothing will be working.' She brushed off the metal chair and sat down, smoothing her skirt.

'Of course. That's what Eric said earlier isn't it?'

She nodded slowly and arched an eyebrow,

'Bill said that we should plan to be doing security duties from tomorrow, like patrolling the perimeter to deter thieves.'

'Really. So, the security men are unionised staff I guess,' I said. 'I'd better get some overalls rather than another suit,' I laughed self-consciously.

'Pardon?' said Anita.

'Oh nothing, long story,' I said, regretting saying it. 'I thought I might be heroically resolving disputes or averting strikes rather than acting as a security guard.'

Anita laughed, 'In your dreams.'

We both looked round as Jim came in with another man, Bill Budd, the Senior Personnel Officer who had interviewed me for the job. Bill was about thirty and looked like a young Rod Stewart with a drooping moustache and feathered haircut.

'Jim's just updated me on your narrow escape this morning,' said Bill grinning.

'It unfortunately sounds like the stewards blame the company rather than the government but give me your notes when you've typed them up.'

'It was pretty hairy, scrabbling around in the dark like a burglar,' I said.

'Well, the good news is that you, Anita and Jim are going to the union mass meeting on the strike vote. It will be at Speke football ground, you'll be listening in from the top of the hill behind the main stand.'

I looked across at Anita, who seemed as alarmed as me.

'You're taking the mick…' I said.

'No, deadly serious this, but this time you'll be on public display so they'll see you, they might even give you a welcome "fuck off personnel" over the microphone.'

Jim laughed, but Bill continued with a serious face,

'Everyone in personnel needs to plan to be doing twelve-hour security shifts from 6 a.m. in the morning and then 6 p.m. in the evenings, alternating weekly. It means you will be crossing the picket lines too. Ok?'

Anita sighed, 'Crossing picket lines. Great. Does that mean we will be spat at and jostled like the miners and dockers?'

Bill cut across her. 'No, you use the inside perimeter fence management car park in strike situations so you cross the picket line in your car. If there's any damage to your car, the company will pick up the bill.'

'That's a bonus,' I said trying to be funny. 'I definitely need a new driver's door, so let's hope they kick that one in.'

'Ha. Well, it's pretty good humoured normally, but not always. The bastards,' said Jim, turning round to leave.

'The van factory down south, and the engine plant in Wales have already gone on strike, so our vote's a formality,' said Bill as he followed Jim out.

Anita and I sipped the lukewarm coffee and looked at each other. We were lost in our own thoughts about what we'd just heard. Anita rummaged in her handbag, giving me the opportunity to stare. What drove a girl to work in this industrial environment I wondered? I managed to stop myself from directly asking her where she was from, and how she'd got here.

She looked up and saw me staring. 'What?' she said, slightly aggressively.

'Oh nothing,' I said.

'Well at least we won't have to run round asking individual staff if they are prepared to work, like we do with unofficial strikes,' she said. 'I'm not sure if it's an official strike though.'

'Not necessarily,' I said, anxious to show I was not a complete greenhorn. 'Unions like to avoid calling strikes official so they don't have to pay strike pay.'

Bill's head appeared round the door, 'Off you pop you two. Public Relations just rang down to say ITV and the BBC will be at the vote, along with that militant local MP, what's his name. Don't get yourselves on TV and you are not authorised to say anything on behalf of the company just in case they approach you. Got that?'

Bill smoothed his moustache and left. I followed Anita out towards Jim's car. Anita's coat was a smart brown camel hair affair, a far cry from my own shabby overcoat. I got in the back of Jim's new Ford Cortina, with its metallic silver paint and black vinyl roof, leaving the front seat free for Anita. She really is gorgeous, I thought. We drove out of the factory gates and as we turned right, I noticed the grim council estate over the road, shuttered shops with graffiti and rubbish blowing everywhere. I looked away out of a strange respect; I'd grown up on one.

I decided I wasn't that nervous about this new task. I'd only met Jim today but he'd showed this morning he knew what he was doing, and he must have had years of strike experience. We drove on through the damp terraced backstreets of Liverpool towards the football ground. Leaving the car parked on some waste ground, we climbed the hill behind the main stand of the tiny stadium. I was surprised to see hundreds of staff being addressed over a PA system by two men who, Jim said, were the Body and Assembly Plants Union Convenors.

'And a warm welcome to the management lackeys who've joined us at the top of the hill.' A loud jeer went up from the workers and many turned and gave V signs.

Jim laughed and waved back as Anita and I instinctively ducked down behind the advertising boards.

'First time I've been called a management lackey,' I said to Anita. 'It's like I've joined the wrong side or something.'

'Better than being called an uppity black twat,' said Anita.

I stared at her, 'Who called you that?'

'Oh, a steward last week when I suggested he was worse than useless in a disciplinary hearing.'

'Bloody hell,' I exclaimed. We gazed down at the meeting. The Labour MP was speaking, fragments of his speech drifting in the wind up to the top of the hill.

'Brothers, we've accepted three years of pay constraint with this unfair social contract, but Liverpool has had enough… the company is hiding behind it… it made huge profits last year. The company's saying the government will take sanctions against it if it breaks this unjust income policy, do not listen to their lies.'

We gradually lost interest with the fragments of rhetoric we could hear, and when it came to the show of hands on taking strike action, it took thirty seconds, and no one voted against. I was surprised the staff were unanimous in their voting and after watching the crowd disperse, we scrambled down the hill to Jim's car. I was shocked to see one of the convenors who had been speaking waiting by the car.

'Willie,' said Jim.

'This yon new apprentice?' looking dismissively at me, he passed a brown envelope to Jim and walked off.

'What did the convenor give you there then, Jim?' queried Anita in an innocent voice.

'Match tickets,' tapping his nose.

I was nonplussed. I sat back in the plush velour upholstery, it was my first day in the job what did I know?

We drove back to the factory. Built in the 1960s, it was a half-mile stretch of light brick buildings, with aluminium extensions jutting out everywhere. We parked up and went to brief Bill Budd, who as the Senior Personnel Officer had a much nicer office in the front office block rather than the piggeries. The previous good humour had drained away from both Bill and Jim. They were gloomy that the government pay policies issue made this different from a normal pay dispute which the company could manage on its own.

'You might as well go home, there's nothing working now and you all need to be in for 6 a.m. sharp,' said Bill. We said our goodbyes. I decided to look in on the idle factory; no production lines were moving, but the lights still shone and groups of supervisors were sitting around chatting. Apart from the occasional hiss of compressed air from the abandoned tools, it was quiet. I sighed and headed for the car park. My car was an old blue VW Beetle that had cost peanuts at college, it was a poor starter and the source of continual anxiety. I turned the ignition, praying it would start and it just about clattered into life. I held the top of the wheel with relief and wondered how a first day at work could be so bizarre.

I drove towards Gateacre, a Liverpool suburb where I'd subleased a council flat from a college friend. The radio news headlines were full of the Ford strike, it was being seen as the first serious challenge to the Labour government pay policy. The first-floor flat was dismal. I had a mattress on the floor and a bookshelf consisting of a plank of wood laid across some bricks. It was freezing, my friend had said not to turn the underfloor heating on as the bills were crazy, and the carpet prevented the heat working anyway. I turned on my old black and white portable TV. The local news showed the strike vote, and I could just see myself far away on the hill. Fame at last, I thought. I made a filter jug of coffee and sat looking over the car park behind the flat. I could have left school at fifteen if I'd wanted to do security duties, I mused. I dozed off, exhausted, waking an hour later in the cold darkness. It would have to be a Chinese takeaway for dinner, sweet and sour pork and chips. Thinking over the day, I dismissed my concern over the fiasco in the canteen – after all, it had all worked out ok. But I still felt uncomfortable about being seen as a management lackey. I knew that by just taking the job, my left-wing college friends had already accused me of selling out, but this was really in the face. A management lackey with no proper bed, ice on the inside of the flat windows and a car where I had to bring the battery in at night. I made a mental note to visit a scrapyard, the car needed a new regulator, and I could see to it on Saturday if I wasn't working a security shift.

— 2 —

Picket line

It was the first day of the all-out strike so while shaving with hot water from the kettle I worried about crossing the picket line. I'd been on plenty of college rent strikes, and anti-fascist demonstrations as a student activist and member of the Broad Left. I thought back to the one or two demos which had got violently out of hand, where the police were involved. Now, for the first time ever I was firmly on the other side of the fence and I felt repulsed by it. Rationally it was part of my new job and my new life. I had better get used to it or just bloody quit and stop feeling sorry for myself.

Approaching the main factory gate, I was sweating and gripped the wheel stiffly. It was a shock to see so many pickets in donkey jackets standing around cooking sausages on 45-gallon oil drum braziers. When they spotted me, the pickets spread out and blocked the road. I held my breath as they stared through the car windows. A shout of 'scab, scab, scab' arose as they gave me the V sign. The senior manager who was operating the barrier from inside the security office slid open the security lodge window and called out, 'Lads, it's our new personnel trainee, tell him to get a decent car!'

The pickets laughed and banged on the roof of my old car and let me through into the management car park. I knew they weren't really interested in me, were there to stop deliveries of car parts and the like, but I was still relieved there was no trouble. My hands were shaking; crossing the picket line felt like a betrayal of my principles and I wasn't sure I was ready for it.

I walked back to the security lodge. Jim and Anita were already there, along with half a dozen others, and introduced me to John May, the press shop manager, ex-Dagenham site, who was managing the situation.

'A lot of you are new to strikes,' John said, 'so here's the brief. At all times there'll be two people patrolling the perimeter fence in a car with a walkie-talkie looking for fence gaps and thieves stealing parts. No confrontations if you see anyone at it. Ring through and we'll involve the police. Another two will be on continuous patrol walking the factory, checking fire hydrant pressures and roof leaks. That leaves the senior manager in charge, me today, and one other always in the security lodge. When the cars run out of fuel you go and get a new one from final assembly testing. There're bacon butties in the canteen at eleven o'clock, the Canteen Manageress is un-unionised thank God. Frank, you don't know the factory yet so Jim'll show you round till you get an idea of the layout.'

The factory was eerie, almost silent, as Jim and I walked around. I had a notebook and drew a map of the locations of key operations. I'd worked as a welder in Vauxhall's before I went to college so knew the basics like framing, subassembly and rough discing. When they got to the assembly and paint plant, it was all new to me, but this would not be part of my personnel patch anyway; I just needed the essentials for the security duties. It was common sense as it was obvious where engines, axles and seats were added to the cars. When it came to the press shop with its massive 1000-ton presses, I was used to that too, my Dad having been a press operator for twenty-five years. The presses looked like a scene from *War of the Worlds*, with names like Schuler and Vickers emblazoned on the sides in huge letters. Jim pointed out the long metal safety poles holding the presses open, as they worked on eccentric shafts that could turn over and crush a man even when switched off.

By now, it was time to go over to the canteen; on the way, I asked Jim why there were no foremen or general foreman in during the strike.

'They're white collar monthly paid like us, but they won't cross picket lines like, even though the general foreman is one grade higher than us. Bastards. To the blue-collar staff, we're all management, but to senior management the foremen are "production" management. We're "proper" management, like ununionized.'

I thought this through and smiled to myself. Yes, industrial relations reality in one line and I was now 'proper' management, even if I was paid flyshit as a trainee. We collected two trays of bacon butties covered in foil and went back to the security lodge. When we opened the door, Anita and John May were slumped on seats looking pale.

'You two look the colour of boiled shite,' said Jim in his inimitable style, putting down the butties.

'We just drove off a container bay and wrecked a car,' said Anita, looking flustered, her head almost between her knees.

'We? You mean you. I'm calling her Anita Knievel here on in,' said John, and a burst of laughter went round the room. I offered him a bacon butty.

'How about me?' Anita asked forcefully. There was an ominous silence as eyes turned to Anita. I was embarrassed and said, 'I didn't think you would eat bacon…'

'I'm not a bloody Pakistani, you wally.'

I could feel myself blushing but John just continued as if nothing had happened saying,

'The car's a right mess, lucky we had our belts on though. To be fair to Knievel, we need the lights on at the back of the container bays, we could see fuck all. Pardon my French.'

I gritted my teeth and sat down next to Anita saying, 'Are you all right, you look well shaken up?'

'Yes, I must be in shock.'

'How's the car?' I regretted saying it as soon as it had come out of my mouth.

Anita frowned at me, shook her head, and looked down.

'We left it with steam coming out, but it didn't catch fire. I'll be alright in a minute. Here have this, I hate bacon.'

I felt I was going red again but was saved by Jim this time.

'Ok Frank, our turn for the car patrol. Let's see if we can get one fitted with crash bars…'

Everyone laughed, except Anita who maintained a serious look. I was glad to be leaving the security lodge.

Jim and I walked back past the piggeries and turned left, heading towards final assembly. Jim explained in his laconic way that some bright spark had got a maximum pay out from the company Suggestion Scheme, just for reducing the fuel put in cars to half a gallon at the end of the line. 'Bloody travesty,' he loudly muttered, 'means we'll be lucky to get an hour's driving before we need to go back for another car,' he said. We got into a light blue Escort and Jim drove out and went clockwise round the huge perimeter road. I just sat quietly, basking in the new car smell. I didn't think I'd actually ever been in a brand-new car before.

After a while, Jim pulled over. He was staring at a piece of damaged perimeter chain fence.

'I thought some bastard's cut that, but it looks like a stacker truck has reversed into it and bent it'.

We drove on and after a while I asked Jim if he thought the professional qualification for personnel officers was worth doing at night school, as I knew little about personnel work.

'We had someone did it at Liverpool Poly last year, there was no time off and he only got his fees paid after he passed, not before mind. Mean bastards our company. He said most of the people on it were from the local council.'

I thought about the boring prospect of studying personnel management at night school until Jim pulled up at the 'magic mushroom,' a giant water tower that was a landmark for miles around. It contained all the water to run the site's fire sprinkler system and we were to check that the chains on the valves were still in place. We swopped drivers, and I was chuffed to be driving a new car, though I never got higher than third gear. I could just see the container bays at the back of the factory where Anita had had her moment. There must have been thirty of them.

We eventually got back to the lodge and I reflected on my first ever shift. There were only six pickets left round the brazier, the others had gone. John said that all the supply lorries had long finished trying to deliver parts and I guessed with the factory at a standstill, the company didn't want them anyway.

When I got home that night after twelve hours I was knackered. I cooked a Fray Bentos pie with oven chips and sat looking out over the uninspiring car park at the back of the council flats while it heated. I was still puzzling about my journey from fringe activist at university to management lackey. Was it only last year that I'd been on the Lewisham anti-National-Front march? Did I still have a piece of the Birmingham National Front banner I'd proudly torn down? Had I really been to the 'Rock against Racism' concert with the Tom Robinson Band in London?

I had a swig from a bottle of Newcastle Brown Ale, I hated the stuff and realised now that I had only drunk it to fit in. The idealism I'd read so excitedly about in my teens, the TV pictures of Paris in 1968, the Grosvenor Square stuff in London, it had disappeared completely now. The factionalism and backstabbing within the Labour Government was horrendous to see and the country seemed to be declining before my very eyes. I stared outside, thinking of the recent nationwide humiliations with Denis Healey and the IMF. Now there was even Rolls Royce, Upper Clyde Shipbuilders and British Leyland all running to the taxpayer for money.

I opened a tin of mushy peas. Could the trade unions not see how the huge number of strikes was destroying confidence in the Callaghan administration? Now I was working and not a student, I was ironically part of the so-called British Disease. What a turn up for the books.

The weeks went on in endless monotony, the alternating twelve hour shifts six days a week with the usual five faces. Social conversations had mostly ended, and I had little in common with the football, horse and dog racing obsessions of the production managers.

Anita had long ago been transferred to the other shift, so I was really disappointed that I seldom saw her except for a few minutes at shift changeover. I toyed with the idea of asking her out for a drink, but that moment just never arrived.

I had got into the habit of buying a copy of the *Morning Star* from the pickets in the morning. One day there was a report from the Labour Party conference that the paper was actually siding with car industry management in resisting the Government's pay restraints. The irony of it. However, reading the paper caused me a problem later one shift when I found myself paired up with the personnel manager who I'd met on my first day, the pipe-smoking Yorkshire man, Eric Moore. After we had secured a car from final assembly he'd said, 'Frank, one of the Superintendents is saying you read the *Morning Star* every morning, is that your politics?'

'You must be joking. It's pro-Soviet rubbish, but there's no other papers there, oh, except *Socialist Worker* which doesn't even have any news.'

'Well, good to hear it. When you eventually get to do some real personnel work, just remember there is a significant minority of stewards who see every little dispute as politicising the workers.'

The car suddenly shuddered, running out of petrol. We had no choice but to walk back for another and after so many weeks, the site was beginning to look like a multicoloured scrapyard for abandoned cars. We were on the far side of the site so went via the press shop, where there had been a roof leak and there were rows of body sides in racks rusting badly.

'Will they be able to use those?' I asked.

'No, they'll be scrapped, melted down and restamped,' said Eric having a puff on his pipe.

After we had picked up a horrible custard yellow van, I plucked up the courage to ask about the impact of the strike.

'I did a lot of economics at college, do you think the foreign shareholders will hold this strike against the UK factories when it comes to future investment?'

He looked sideways at me,

'This strike probably not, they can see it's about pay policy, it's political. But the damage has been done by the hundreds of minor strikes we've had over the last few years, their attitudes are already hardened.'

'How do you mean?'

'It's touch and go if the new model, project Arnold, is coming here. But look at the new Fiesta plant in Spain. It's devastating Dagenham Fiesta production, and the Granada and Capri models have just gone to Germany.'

'Have you told our staff about the new model issue, do they know?' I asked.

'The unions are short-sighted, they see all the capital invested here and think they're safe. Some of them even write to the chairman and call for nationalisation without compensation,' he laughed.

'Well, maybe it's just me starting a new job with an indefinite strike but the whole country seems to be in chaos. Everyone seems to be threatening strike action, firemen and social workers this week. If I can see how bad this is with no experience, why can't everyone else?' I said.

Eric looked at me. 'Well, you've caught on quick laddie. Just drive around, the Triumph TR plant is in trouble, Pressed Steel Fisher bodies is, the Leyland truck business. They're going to the wall monthly, I just hope this strike isn't our death rattle too.'

'So, have I joined a sinking ship then?' I asked.

Eric smiled.

'You'll be ok. Do your industrial relations training here, and I'm sure all these strikes will look good on your CV. Anyway, if the worst happens, it'll be many years before an investment this size runs down.'

We pulled over, Eric nodded at me and we went back into the security lodge.

That evening in the flat I felt incredibly low. I knew it was probably a combination of the prognosis on the factory future from the boss, the depressing physical environment and the exhausting twelve-hour shifts. It didn't help that the radio news was blaring out the latest arguments from the ineffectual James Callaghan about the state of the country. I just had to open my front door to see the state of everything, I didn't really need the news. The continual petrol queues because of the tanker drivers' strikes annoyed me the most. Even my university sociology books propped up on bricks seemed pointless – Nicos Poulantzas and Louis Althusser. When I'd read them last year, I'd struggled to see what relevance they had to contemporary Britain. Now, in a society riven by industrial disharmony, I was beginning to think they were just left-wing academics writing for each other. No one in the unions, in management, even in the Labour Party read them. The thought of becoming an academic myself if the job didn't suit, and writing stuff like that, became less attractive by the minute. I was beginning to nod off when the telephone rang.

'Hi Frank, it's me' said Anita. 'I wanted to ask if you're not doing anything tonight, do you fancy some food out?'

'Oh, hi,' I said recovering from the shock of the phone ringing and Anita's voice. 'Yes, that would be great, not sure I'll be great company after five weeks of twelve-hour security duties though.'

'Everybody has had enough, so join the club! I'm off this nightshift so how about in town at the Philharmonic in an hour?'

'Right, the one with the gilded urinals?'

'I wouldn't know,' she laughed.

I was over the moon at the invitation on such a grey weekday night. I knew a change of scene would cheer me up, and I could get to know Anita and her probably interesting background. I unplugged the car battery from the charger and thumbed through the Liverpool A to Z to check where I was going before I set off. As I drove into town it struck me again how down at heel Liverpool looked. When I'd arrived earlier in the year, I'd done some of the main touristy sights. I particularly remembered the bleak view from the tower of the imposing Anglican cathedral. Many streets still looked bomb damaged from the war, with scrapyards and car parks on waste ground that had not been restored. I parked up, making sure nothing was on show as Liverpool really was the car theft capital of England. I smirked at the thought that my car might be stolen as even kids wouldn't be seen dead in it. It was hardly a 1600E Cortina, the thieves' favourite.

— 3 —

Zorbas

Anita was already in the Philharmonic bar when I got there. I had only met her on the occasional shift changeover when our paths crossed in the security lodge. I was worried that I'd appear academic, even 'snooty,' as one manager had called me. He had said that I seemed to care a lot about politics, unions and the state of the country but not much about people, which he said was odd for someone intending to work in personnel. He also said I seemed switched off from the normal security lodge banter.

'Hiya. Do you want another one of those?' I said smiling at her choice of drink.

'Yep, Babycham please.' I came back with one and a pint of John Smith's.

'I thought only grannies in bingo halls still drank that.'

'I know, never lost the taste of my youth. Well, I have to say you look pretty tired, bags under the eyes at your age?'

'Yeah,' I said, 'I'm really drained by these twelve-hour security shifts and then having to listen to superintendents rabbit on about football, horses and bloody golf. I can't seem to sleep during the day when I am on nightshift, it's really wearing me out. Anyway, that's enough of me wallowing in my misery, how have you been finding security duties?'

Anita smiled. 'I certainly know Jim and Bill better, I could tell you their wives' ages and their kids' birthdays.'

We both laughed warmly at our colleagues. The pub was lively and bright with old-fashioned Victorian velvet wallpaper and beautiful ceilings.

27

'I've been meaning to ask, you know you said you were a Ugandan Asian, does that mean you were thrown out by Idi Amin a few years ago?'

Anita looked slightly taken aback.

'Yes, I was about thirteen when we left, nice well-off family with maids and servants, landing in a small flat over a shop in Leicester.'

'Where did you get your posh accent from then?'

'Privately educated colonial school till I was thirteen I guess, tell me when the interrogation has finished?'

'Sorry, I can get a bit intense but one last question, honest. How did you end up working in a car factory?' Anita leaned back on the soft sofa, extended her legs with the Babycham in one hand. She smoothed down her trouser suit and casually said, 'My family worked long hours to establish some corner shops in Leicester, I just wanted to try a large business, kind of contrast it with what I had grown up with. Eventually I did an MBA, there was a choice to specialise in marketing or personnel and it seemed a more natural fit for me. That's it.'

Anticipating what Anita might say and never that happy talking about my background, I got up to get another round of drinks in.

'Hold on, my turn,' and Anita slithering back up like a snake. 'I don't like being in debt to anyone,' she smiled, and went to the bar. I sat back down, slightly miffed, not by a girl going Dutch but the 'not being in debt' remark. When she came back, she looked at me expectantly.

'And?'

'Umm, nothing interesting at all, council house, comprehensive, late mum mostly a housewife, my dad a press operator in a car factory in Luton. Oh, I worked as a welder in the car factory before I went to college.'

Anita looked surprised.

'Ah, that explains why you seem to know so much about car factories without seeing our one actually working...'

There was a sudden crash, we looked up to see two guys throwing punches and shouting at each other only two tables away. I stood quickly, helped Anita up and said 'Let's go in case they start throwing bottles.'

Holding Anita's arm firmly, my eyes never left the fight till we were outside, walking away.

'I'm starving. Shall we get something to eat? There's a nice Greek in Hardman Street that does great retsina and kebabs,' I said. Anita left her arm hooked in mine and I covertly looked at her as we strolled up the noisy street.

'Phew, I've never seen a fight break out that fast before. Oh, "Zorbas", it's really called "Zorbas", she laughed pointing at the sign.

'I know, you really couldn't make it up,' as we went in and got a table for two overlooking the street.

'Thanks for suggesting we meet, by the way,' I said. 'You're the only person my age I've met so far in this job.'

'Well, as we were saying in the pub, the strike can't go on forever, and you don't know what the job actually is yet do you? You'll soon be a really old hand like me, with a year's personnel rather than security experience…' she laughed .

The retsina was cold and sharp, it made my eyes water.

'If security is work, God help me,' I said, raising my glass and tinkling it with Anita. It was hard to avoid noticing how attractive Anita was, with her petite figure and smart clothes. I looked away, it was seven months since my acrimonious split with my girlfriend. We chatted for another hour, discussing the state of the nation, the car industry, immigration, and our work colleagues. I had just enough self-awareness to not trust my instincts with women but thought we got on well. We were both on the morning shift for once, so we left at nine just as the restaurant was filling up. I felt like thanking her again for inviting me out, as it had really cheered me up. It sounded too fawning, so I didn't. We departed for our cars, I looked back at Anita before praying my car would actually start, which it did.

Autumn became winter. Reading the newspapers in the lodge during security duties, I was staggered to see the firemen had got a 22% pay increase and then the heating engineers had got a 30% staged deal. These were huge figures and the TUC had finally rejected the Labour government's joint economic statement so it looked like the country might descend into further chaos. Much of the talk in the security lodge was now about when our company would cave in to the union's demands as the strike had been going on over eight weeks. After two months, the strike ended with a pay deal. It broke government guidelines and everyone dreaded what that might mean for the future of the factory.

— **4** —

Pram

For me, the first day back after the strike and the first day in my real job started with a short meeting for all personnel staff convened by the personnel manager. He'd arranged the meeting to warn that the Prime Minister had spoken in the House of Commons, threatening economic sanctions against the company for breaking the government pay policy.

The media were reporting that public servants, BBC technicians and oil tanker drivers were threatening strike action over the pay policy. It was clear the Ford pay deal was the one the government really needed to defeat if it was to maintain its policy. The country was feeling feverish, on the verge of disorder. During the rest of that month, I sat in with Jim, learning how he handled disputes, recruitment, sickness absence and the like. It was obvious that Jim did a lot of 'deals', as many a time I would be sent out for coffee to find on return that it was 'all sorted', with no details ever forthcoming. After over six weeks mostly with Jim, I was regarded as fully trained up.

My first difficult job came after a couple of months, one nightmare of a Thursday night. Most of the blue-collar staff chose to be paid cash weekly, and I was back on nightshift, on my own as my induction was formally over. The handling of 'advance of wages' interviews with workers who had unexpected bills and short-term money difficulties was known locally as 'subs.' They wanted cash that would be taken out of the following week's wages, so this required a personnel officer or two at the factory from 10 p.m. till 12 midnight on a Thursday.

Having been on a 'subs' night with Jim a couple of times, I had formed the view that some of the workers were just feckless, and had spent their wages betting on the dogs and down the pub. I thought the practice was seriously old-fashioned, and that staff should be paid in the bank so they could then ask their bank for an overdraft rather than making up cock and bull stories for a Thursday night. I was seriously reluctant to come back and do it but was told by my boss that I had to take part in the rota.

Lenny Lobo, a volatile mixed-race shop steward in one of my areas was waiting for me as I came in on the night 'subs' shift.

'Mr Thomas, this is err, Derek from the body in white area. The thing is his Judy had her pram nicked last week from outside his front door so he needs twenty-five quid for a new one.' I couldn't stop myself from laughing out loud.

'Lenny, I must have done twenty subs in my short time here, that's the tallest story I've ever heard. No way.'

'Eh, are youse callin' me a liar?'

Derek, an unhealthy-looking teenager intervened, 'Lenny, it's alright. There's nottin' down for us.'

'I didn't call you a liar, I just don't believe the case for a sub and I don't think he does either,' looking at Derek. Lenny went apoplectic, stood up and shouted at me, 'Youse got thirty minutes to change yuh mind or I'm blowin' the whistle. I'm not havin' a snotty nosed young personnel git callin' me a liar, gorrit la? Derek, back to framin' now.' They both stood up and walked out, Lenny slamming the door.

I was shocked by the outburst but kept busy by a new starter sub and a final gas cut-off demand, both of which I agreed to. The door opened, Lenny put his head in and said, 'Yes or no?'

'No.' I said with a lump in my throat.

It was nearly midnight, the subs queue had gone, so I opened the factory door a few yards away from my office to listen. I felt sick as the distinct blast of a football whistle blowing could be heard, the normal call for an unofficial walk out, a 'wildcat' strike. I retreated into my office to see if staff would respond, stoically determined not to be bullied by a shop steward. I stared at the green desk phone expecting it to ring. Instead, the door opened and the nightshift production manager, Bill Ryman, was standing there. He was a white-haired red-faced cockney who I'd met on security duties. In the best of times, he was a bully, always contrasting how great the Dagenham factory was compared with Liverpool. This was not the best of times.

'You're fuckin' shittin' me, aren't you? I've lost five cars in the time it's taken to walk here, cos you won't give some scouse twat a fuckin' sub?'

I was outraged at being sworn at by a senior manager and being told what to do.

'He's lying about the pram and baby clothes, and I'm not being bullied by a steward so I'm not signing off a sub,' and stared icily back at him.

'I don't care whether it's bollocks or not.' He reached into his pocket, pulling out some notes. He slammed his hand on the desk. ''Ere's the fuckin' money. I'll pay, I'm not losing thirty-six cars an hour and I'll be naming you as the cause of the fuckin' loss.'

'I'm not authorising it,' I said as sternly as I could.

'We've just lost nine weeks' production with the pay strike, are you goin' to tell our boss we're losing more cos of a fuckin' pram?'

I took a deep breath, I realised my gamble that Lenny would not actually call a walk out over a sub had backfired. I was beginning to feel queasy and decided to ring Bill Budd at home for advice. Thankfully, he answered, I explained the situation and Bill asked to speak to Bill Ryman.

They spoke and then Bill Ryman handed the phone back to me and left.

'I'll authorise the sub so you don't lose face and we'll discuss it tomorrow. Ok?'

I was bitterly disappointed, but rationally understood the decision. There was no way out, they really were losing cars. I signed the subs sheet in Bill Budd's name, gave it to the pay office and went home. I had a sleepless night, tossing and turning about the car losses but was determined to argue the case the next day. I wondered if I might be asked to leave.

Not surprisingly, I found a note on my desk to report to Bill Budd's office in the front office block. Bill had recruited me. Sitting next to him was Eric Moore, the industrial relations manager.

'You know Frank', said Eric, 'we've never had a labour relations officer cited in a stoppage report for the loss of twenty-four cars before.'

'Yes but…'

'Look, you might well have been technically right. He might have been lying, who knows? But you can't have an intellectual view of your job, well intentioned as it might be. This is a dirty business, the stewards have power and you don't. They're now threatening to black you. If they do, it will be the end of your career here.'

I felt nauseous, I could see my career burning in flames before it had even really started.

Eric leaned forward and said, 'It's like this. We need the cars after the strike, and we need the new model investment for next year. If we didn't need the cars, like an old model run out, you would be saving the company money but you're not.'

'So, it's like some kind of guerrilla war then, they kick us when we're down and we kick them when we're up?' I replied.

I regretted going that far, but Eric ignored the comment anyway. 'Am I blacked then?'

'No, the deal is we've agreed you're on an interpersonal relations training course next week. Handling emotions, compromising, that kind of stuff. Listen, this is difficult industrial relations in a closed shop and if you can't get on with the stewards you need to think of other options. Oh, and Lenny Lobo has had a right bollocking from the convenor for blowing the whistle without putting in a grievance, but you don't know that.' Eric then looked down at his paperwork and I realised I was dismissed.

'By the way', he added as I left the room, 'Bill insisted your name was removed from the stoppage report. Anyone in Head

Office who had seen that you personally had cost twenty-four cars would probably have sent you your cards. Consider yourself lucky.'

I turned that over in my mind, as I walked, humiliated, back to the shitty office in the piggeries. I looked round at the yellow walls and sighed.

Jim O'Neill walked in grinning.

'Respect man. Bloody hell. You've got some balls. Hey, Anita come and listen to this.'

'What?' she enquired.

'Meet the legend in the making, Fruitcake Frank the Pramlad, the whole of the body plant knows him now. There'll be no queue outside his door on subs night!'

'Tell me later, I've got an absence meeting,' said Anita looking puzzled.

'Jim, piss off and leave me in peace,' I said. Jim left still grinning. A few moments later there was a knock on the door. I looked up to see Lenny Lobo march in. I stood up warily but was surprised to see Lenny offer his hand, so I shook it suspiciously.

'Err, I might 'ave been a bit hasty yesterday, like, but he's the genuine article and he did lose his pram. No hard feelings.'

I looked closely at him, he seemed to be serious. 'I was beginning to think the same, maybe I was hasty too. How am I going to know what a tall story is and what's genuine? I'm not signing off every cock and bull story, they'll have to sack me first.' I thought for a moment. 'Look. If you have cases where you know it's going to sound bullshit but it's true, come and see me beforehand and we'll discuss it. It might avoid this grief in future anyway.'

'Okey doke. I'll do that, a deal.'

We shook hands. 'I've gotta go, I'm doin' toilet reliefs.' Lenny left as quickly as he'd arrived. I wished I smoked. Instead, I went and got a coffee and shut the door. I said out loud 'industrial relations, 1978 Great fucking Britain.' I looked down at my desk diary, I had a meeting in ten minutes on a disciplinary hearing for unauthorised absence. 'Shit, shit, shit.'

Alco Judy

One day there was a knock at the door and a shop steward called Benny walked in; he was from forklift trucks/production control so not my personnel area.

'Err, Mr Pramlad, Lenny said you might be the only one that can help me out,' he said.

'With what?' I asked suspiciously, trying not to smile at my new nickname.

'I'm doin' a worker's education course on politics, and I have to write an essay once a month. I left school at fifteen to work on Garston Docks like, so I'm all in with worry.'

I laughed.

'You're tight you are,' he winged, standing up.

'Sit down. What's the title then?' Benny took out a piece of paper from his bib and tucker overalls and read it out.

'Is Trotsky's concept of permanent revolution relevant to post-industrial Britain?'

I laughed again, so loud that Anita heard it in the office next door and looked through the glass partition between our offices.

'Come back at lunchtime and I'll work on a few ideas with you.'

'Right dere t'anks, you're a good skin you are,' and Benny left.

Anita walked in as soon as Benny left, as nosy as ever.

'Well, why was one of my stewards seeing you and what was so funny then?'

'You won't believe it. Benny, wants me to help him write an essay on Trotsky!'

'For his union education course? Do you know anything about Trotsky then?' she enquired.

'Yes, I studied him for two years.'

'You're full of surprises.' Anita pulled the door to on the way out; a few moments later she looked through the partition again, shaking her head and smiling. It took me fifteen minutes to put down some bullet points for and against Trotsky and his relevance to 1978 Britain (none in my view). Just as I finished, Lenny Lobo strolled in.

'Alright, la. Ta for sortin' Benny, he's a pain in the jaxi with his course.'

'I'll be interested to see if he gets a worse mark with my ideas' I said.

'He'll be a no mark either way,' smirked Lenny.

'Frank, you know you said youse never been to a match.'

'Yeah.'

'I've gorra spare ticket against West Ham this Saturday if you're interested, like?'

I thought fast, I wasn't sure if that was Everton or Liverpool playing.

'Great. I'd love to.'

'Ok, two o'clock my house, we'll be in the Kop so roll up yer footy echo.'

'What's that mean?' I said.

'Don't bring your best whistle.'

'Right,' I said a little dubiously, as Lenny handed over a scrap of paper with his address on it and breezed out as quickly as he'd arrived.

It was usual for new graduate trainees to spend ten minutes with the overall site manager within three months of joining the company. Bill described it as a 'cross between a career chat and a rant about employee relations.'

Herman Neustadt, the site manager was a German electrical engineer by training. Known to everyone as Herman the German, he was in his mid-fifties on assignment from the sister plant in Germany. One of his two secretaries showed me into the outer office before I was led into his inner sanctum, a massive room with rosewood panelling and leather chairs round a table set with china cups on a tray. He looked very stressed and I didn't know whether I should offer to come back another time.

'Aach so, you read Sociology and Political Theory and now you're here, in employee relations? You're the same age as my son, he is a circus performer in Belgium, but my daughter is an engineer. What a world it is. Now, explain to me how I tell my American boss that we lost 134 cars midweek to a Liverpool–Everton football derby match. He thinks we have made some kind of mess of our leave planning,' he laughed.

'I agree it's a disaster that so many staff put going to a match ahead of their jobs. It's something to do with the whole history of the Liverpool docks work culture. I have no excuses, I think the unions should help us sort it out instead of defending the staff at disciplinary hearings. It makes me sick.'

'You know,' he said, 'I was brought up in a docks culture too, Hamburg during the war – it was a worse place to be than Liverpool. I manned an anti-aircraft gun as a fifteen-year-old during the bombing raids in 1944, it was the Americans by day and the British by night, and it still gives me nightmares thirty years later. I never resolved whether it was the experience of near starvation in the rebuilding of our country after the war or something in the German character that has led to us outperforming you British in manufactured goods. I cannot remember the last strike in a German car factory.' He continued, 'On my first holiday in the Black Forest after the war, I fell in love with British motorbikes like Norton and Matchless which were ridden by the British army, one kind soldier had given me a pillion ride! They were the best in the world and one reason I'd learnt English and became an Anglophile. Now, a strange worker's cooperative called Norton Villiers Triumph makes appalling quality Nortons, it is a great shame.'

'I know, I've just bought a Kawasaki 250 triple instead of a British bike, there's no comparison.'

'Aah, a fellow biker, good. The Japanese are excellent engineers like us Germans. I sometimes think your car industry will follow the biking industry into oblivion. But soon I will return to Germany, and I will take with me a BSA Gold Star that I have just bought, the pinnacle of British engineering. I intend to retire to the Black Mountains and potter around thinking of what might have been.'

His eyes screwed up. 'Anyway, enough nostalgia, anything you can do to stop the stupid wildcat strikes the better, although it will be too late for me. If this plant is to have a future it has to have the new car and van model.'

Back in my office, I had a disciplinary case to deal with. In only one of the six disciplinaries that I'd done with Lenny Lobo, the Body in White steward, had he been to lobby me before the hearings. This was a persistent lateness case where a door hanger called Peter Barrett had already had verbal, written and final warnings for not turning up on time for the shift start. Because he worked on the moving production line hanging car and van doors, it meant the line couldn't get going until a relief man was found to do the job. Lenny himself had covered for him several times and there had been car losses. The lad had a final warning three months ago and was really 'due his cards', dismissal. No extenuating circumstances had ever been mentioned, he'd apologised at all the hearings, but the management view was that he was never going to change and was bone idle.

Today, Lenny had been in and said that Barrett had told him that with his job at risk he was prepared to tell the truth. The truth was that his wife was an alcoholic. After almost a year of trying to help her, he'd finally been given a date for her to be admitted to a rehab clinic from next week and he could guarantee his early shift starts from here on in. I asked Lenny if he believed the guy, he'd said that on his daughters' lives he did. If Lenny believed it, I would have to believe it, that was our deal and he had never let me down to date. This meant a trip to see the dismissing manager, who unfortunately on this shift was the cockney bully Bill Ryman.

'He's had four fuckin' chances, he's gettin' no more. Period. Now do your job, leave me in peace.'

I continued regardless. 'I want us to do a one off, guaranteed not to be used as a precedent in any other lateness cases. I'm calling it a 'final, final warning' due to confidential circumstances in this individual case.'

'What the fuck is that?'

I stood there, standing up to Bill and arguing. Eventually Bill, worn down by my persistence and anxious to get rid of me from his office reluctantly agreed.

'If this goes tits up, you're for the fuckin' high jump. You still owe me twenty-five fuckin' cars from your last cockup.' Back in my piggery's office, it wasn't long before Bill Budd called me into his office as Bill Ryman had told him about my proposed arrangement. He looked closely at me and made it clear that he'd backed me up but I would be severely admonished by Eric Moore if my 'extra one-off step in this case' actually did become custom and practice across the site.

Later that day, Willie John, the tough Scottish Body Plant Convenor who was the leading steward, put his head round the door carrying a plastic bucket. He had the reputation of a wily old fox who could be a nasty bit of work, but at least had no hidden political agenda.

'There's a laddie in the press shop whose son's got leukaemia and we're collectin' to send him to Disneyland.' I had quickly discovered that Liverpudlians would collect for anybody. I had never been anywhere where there was such a community sense of charity. But they never seemed to trust national charities and most of the collections were for family crises or local hospices. I had begun to quietly admire and support them in my few months there, so I put some coins in. On the way out, Willie John said, 'We know youse stickin' your neck out for that lad with the alco Judy.' He grinned and left before I could reply. The Peter Barrett alcoholic wife meeting went well, my proposal was accepted, and I had gained some credibility with Lenny and the other stewards since my pram subs disaster and it was thankfully not being discussed as a future precedent.

That afternoon, the 2 p.m. shift in the paint shop never showed up which meant car bodies could not move and the factory ground to a complete halt. I stood up and looked for Anita in case she knew more, but she wasn't in. Thankfully, I bumped into the Welfare PO Johnnie Murphy who, as a retired shop steward, seemed to know everything whenever there was a strike.

'Shite money,' said Johnnie, then 'dirt money,' he offered as further explanation when he realised I didn't understand. It turned out to be about the paid time that the paint shop workers were given to change into and out of clean overalls. So that was another 300 cars lost, never to be recovered.

Saturday dawned wet and cold as I made my way to Scotland Road to meet up at Lenny Lobo's neat, terraced house. Some of the houses in the road were boarded up, with old prams and rubbish in their front yards. There were streets and streets of the houses. I was surprised, though I didn't know why, when Lenny's wife Leanne turned out to be a white blonde with a heavy scouse accent. Two beautiful girls bounded up and Leanne offered me foil wrapped sandwiches to put in my pocket.

'No, I couldn't, I was going to treat Lenny for getting the tickets.' I said. She laughed and smiled with flashing eyes,

'He said youse was a bit simple, a bit naive like.' I blushed. Was that how I was seen by the stewards?

'Put 'em in an inside pocket, youse never get your hands to an outside pocket in the Kop.'

Lenny appeared, kissed his wife and daughters and we moved towards the door.

'Thanks for the sandwiches,' I shouted backwards towards Leanne.

'Hope you like Spam, we're brassic after nine weeks on strike pay!'

I felt like a fish out of water as we walked along. I'd been to a lot of Luton Town division four matches with my Dad, but never a big division one match. As we got nearer the ground, the crowd magnified and began to funnel and press in on us, reminding me of my days as a student on demos and rent strikes. I began to feel anxious in the large crowd. Lenny said, 'When we're in, we're in, if you want a slash go now...' I did as suggested. I was soon holding onto Lenny as we pushed our way into the Kop end, a few rails for support and standing room only. The noise was deafening, louder than any demo I had been on, my arms were pinned by the crush and I swayed with everyone else as the ball drifted left then right. Any perceived foul or attempt on goal was met with a crescendo of noise and swearing about the referee. It felt like an out of body experience.

'You'll never walk alone...' the crowd sang. Liverpool scored, everyone went delirious and seriously deafened me and I was left with a ringing in the ears. Suddenly, coins, sauce bottles and other rubbish were landing among us, thrown by a bunch of West Ham skinheads. The stewards rushed up to fill the dividing gangway between the rival supporters. The match ended and we had to wait thirty minutes for the away supporters to be cleared out before we could begin to move. Outside, police horses were keeping a small crowd of West Ham supporters away from the Liverpool fans streaming out of the ground. Occasionally, stones and rubbish were thrown at us over the police cordon. The police horses charged the West Ham supporters, with the riders coshing them with long truncheons till they scrambled off.

'Christ, not exactly a family day out,' I shouted with my ears still ringing.

'It's nor always as bad as that,' said Lenny, as we darted into a corner pub, standing between a bombsite and some infill shops. It was heaving with people and had old-fashioned snug-type fittings. I got the pints in and we managed to find a couple of seats to eat our sandwiches, completely squashed as they were.

'Great header dat,' said Lenny, taking a huge swig of the mild beer.

'All I saw was the ball go in the net, I couldn't see who headed it,' and laughed. I looked down at myself, my trousers smelt like someone had pissed on them and I was hot and sweaty with cigarette burns on my coat.

'Not my idea for a Saturday out, but to experience the Kop end, that was something else,' I said to Lenny.

We sat there, reeking of smoke.

'How long you been a repairman then? I asked. I had seen him doing the whole range of jobs from rehanging doors to donning protective masks and discing over the lead joints on the roof joins.

'Last four years, it's difficult to do a line job as a steward with all the time off for meetings and the like.'

'Will you stay?'

'The money's good when we're norra on strike.'

'Do you want to be a senior steward or district official then?'

'Nah. No interest in political shit. Just wanna support the lads when arsehole management get uppity, that's me.' He sat back in his seat with the relaxation which comes only from physical labour.

'Are they really all that bad?' I said.

'Not as bad as when the factory first opened, they thought they could pay us less than Dagenham, and treated us like monkeys. We weren't used to asking permission to get a brew or to go for a slash, like. A lorra people quit after a week as they couldn't stand being treated like machines.'

'Yeah, well Taylorism's the same the world over,' I added.

'What's that?'

'The production system Henry Ford invented, breaking big jobs down into simple, repetitive tasks. One of my lecturers used to say that the Germans or Japanese were better at it than us, as the Brits don't like being told what to do.'

'Well, Herman the German took us to the Ruhr factory last year, for a visit,' said Lenny. 'Germans my arse, all looked like

Turks to me, doing twelve-hour shifts on the lines, not many Germans workin'.'

'My dad used to say that after worrying whether he was going to be torpedoed at night in the war, doing twelve-hour nightshifts in a factory was pretty relaxing.'

'Yeah, well most of us never even did National Service, let alone fight the war. It's either thirty years of this monotony to look forward to or it's Parks and Gardens in the Council. There's nottin' else down for us in Liverpool.' On that note, we drank up and left, with Lenny nodding to various people he knew. I left him outside his house and went back to Gateacre, thinking about the mad day it had been.

It was getting dark as I drove back. Going in the other direction, into town, were old cars with young people playing loud music on their eight tracks. I stopped at the Chinese takeaway near the flat, one couple queuing were dressed to the nines and obviously going clubbing, I was always surprised with the effort many people put into their appearance in Liverpool. I didn't know whether to be as impressed or not with their sangfroid about the long petrol queues at the garage near the flat either. I saw in the papers that the refuse workers had gone on strike too, so the bins were starting to overflow, and crows were fighting over the rubbish. I walked back, put on the portable fan heater to erase the chill, and sat down to eat the takeaway.

I opened a can of Boddingtons and slumped over the Formica table. I knew I wasn't that happy with life but couldn't put my finger on exactly why. It felt like a perfect storm of events outside my control. I was annoyed by the country descending into what amounted to chaos, and the petrol and refuse strikes were becoming more than a pain. The industry I'd chosen to work in seemed to have a difficult future if it had one at all in the long term. Even the job I'd chosen was looked down on by the production managers and engineers and as for the relationships side of it, I wasn't sure I had the character insight for it. I also had no social life to speak of, I was a long way from my college friends except Pete and was lonely. I also now realised that my time-consuming fringe involvement in student politics had meant that I didn't really have any hobbies either.

I tried to be more positive about my life. I was independent with a half-decent job and I was still only twenty-three. I had come from a working-class background and partially transcended it; surely, I should be happy? But where was the enthusiasm, where was the spark? At the moment, it felt like I was in some kind of surviving the week mode and I knew I verged on being permanently miserable. I drifted off to the sound of 'Famous Blue Raincoat' by Leonard Cohen, the melancholy suited my mood.

— 6 —

Sleeping

The months rolled on and before I knew it, I was experienced in the job of employee relations in a personnel department.

One morning, Bill Budd the Senior PO was at my desk, feet up, fiddling with his moustache and smoking a stinking Gauloises cigarette.

'Good morning Frank, a development opportunity has arisen.'

I eyed him, another training course for some transgression, I thought.

'The occupational nurse has been over, she's saying that when she comes in on a morning when the A shift has been on nights, someone has been sleeping in one of her surgery beds.'

I hung my coat on the hat stand and sat down on the visitor side of my desk.

'Right. Like Goldilocks.'

'There's greasy hair stains on the pillow and the bed smells of smoke.'

'It could be you then' I said, looking directly at Bill and trying not to laugh.

'Hoho. You and the new trainee Tim are back on nights, doing subs on Thursday, so after you finish at midnight, you can go over to medical and catch him at it. Just suspend him on the spot and sack him the next day. Got that?'

I thought about it for a moment. 'I'll need a steward and some kind of manager I guess?'

'Find out who he is, then get his foreman over and do the business. Tim has no experience of this kind of thing yet, you've done quite a few dismissals now so show him the ropes.' I sat down on my swivel chair as Bill left, leaving the door open until the smoke dissipated. I felt that was a vote of confidence in me, if nothing else.

Five minutes later Tim walked in. He was older than me, balding, soft faced and clearly privately educated. His family were tea planters in Ceylon. He always seemed to wear clerical grey suits and looked like a fish out of water in a blue-collar factory environment. He was even newer than me and had transferred from the company graduate finance scheme. In the few weeks he'd been there, stewards would go to his office just to hear him speak.

'What ho Frank, do we have a plan for Thursday?'

'Yep. I'll bring a couple of torches, so we don't have to turn the lights on, the keys are being dropped off with us Thursday, that's it.'

'Keys? If it's locked the sleeper must have key access as well then.'

'Umm, good point. That narrows it down a bit. I suppose we could ask that, but then it might tip off the person if they are a key holder. You could pick up a pen and notebook to take down what he says on Thursday as well.'

'Okey doke, this will be interesting,' and he left.

Thursday night subs eventually came, and after the usual array of final demands, eviction notices and sob stories we locked up and had a cup of coffee till the time was right. I couldn't help noticing that the queue to see Tim had been twice as long as mine, it might mean he was seen as a soft touch or me as a hard one. We gathered our torches and with the lights off, sneaked out of the piggeries over towards the health centre.

'Bugger,' I shouted as I banged my knee on a fire extinguisher on the way out of the office. 'God, that hurt, give me a minute,' I moaned.

We eventually walked round to the entrance to the surgery office and found the door open. I whispered to Tim,

'If we go diagonally through here, there's a receptionist office then the nurse's surgery with two beds. We'll turn the torches on to look for the electric light when in there, but not before, ok?' Tim nodded, we were both breathing heavily. There was someone lying on the bed in the gloom, I could hear them snoring heavily. At the count of three, Tim shone the torch and I turned on the light switch. It was clearly a security man, still in his uniform. He woke up, so startled that he banged his head on the wall, and immediately said, 'I felt ill, just had to lie down, must have been something I ate,' he mumbled, blinking from the light. I looked at him intently.

'So, your shift supervisor knows you're here does he?'

'No, didn't have time to tell him.'

'Is that right,' I said. 'You stay there while we get your supervisor and steward over.'

Tim walked the short hop to the security lodge and briefed the supervisor on the way back, a steward unknown to me was also in tow. Both were looking shocked. The guy had removed the blanket by now. We sat him in a chair and gathered round the nurse's desk, he really did look ill with his sewage yellow white hair and gaunt face.

'At 12.25 a.m. Tim and I, acting on a tip off, found you asleep in rather than on, the nurse's bed. You said you had collapsed and had not told your supervisor where you were.'

'That's right,' said the security guard.

'Well, I don't believe you, we know you've done it before, so we are suspending you forthwith for sleeping on duty when supposed to be on patrol. It's potentially gross misconduct, so go home now and be back for 10 a.m. tomorrow, my office, with your steward.' He said nothing more and got up and left with the duty steward, holding his head.

Tim looked at the supervisor and said,

'He was carrying a walkie-talkie, would he not have been in constant contact on patrol?'

'Yes, but there are dead spots around the site though, so I'd probably not miss him for thirty to forty minutes when on patrol. He's been here a lorra years now, a few minor warnings about lateness, not the brightest but not much else.'

'Ok,' I said. We locked up and left. On the way out, I said to Tim, 'We'll need to be in early to write up the incident report and brief Bill, and the guy's senior manager will also need briefing before ten, as he should run the meeting. We can both attend. Ok?'

'See you then,' and we parted ways. As I was walking out, the steward who had been called in to the meeting caught me up.

'Right, I'll tell the convenor tomorrow, I'm not handling a possible dismissal outside my own area. I know there is a vacancy for a steward in security, so he'll have no one like, so Willie John should represent him.' I agreed somewhat reluctantly, as Willie John was always a handful.

The following morning, I briefed Bill, the Senior PO. We agreed that it would be wise that I was not judge and jury on this and that Bill would be the personnel representative managing the meeting, with the security manager chairing. I would take the notes, and Tim, the duty steward, and the shift supervisor would be called as witnesses. Willie John, the convenor, and John, the security man, sat on one side of Bill's big desk. The security manager, Bill and I sat on the other side. Everyone was deathly quiet, recognising the seriousness of the situation.

Bill opened the meeting,

'Now, because sleeping on duty is a serious offence, particularly in a job that ensures the safety of the whole site, we are moving directly to the gross misconduct stage of the disciplinary procedure. Do you understand that John?'

Willie John answered instead,

'Yep.'

The security manager outlined the events of the previous night and was about to call in the witnesses when Willie John put up his hand,

'We don't need no witnesses, there's no dispute o'er what happened. The thing is, youse jumped to the wrong conclusion.

He's been suffering from dizzy spells for a few months when he leaves the lodge for his patrols. Not wishing to cause any fuss, he's just taken the odd nap on the nurse's bed when it came over him, like. He knows now he should have sought medical advice, but he was anxious not to let down his colleagues by making them cover his patrols and most important of all, he'd mentioned it to yon manager.'

I couldn't stop myself snorting in disbelief, which earned a sharp look from both Willie John and Bill. After a long argument about the believability of his story, an adjournment was called by Bill but not before the manager confirmed the security guard had complained about feeling faint occasionally. Bill tore the manager off a strip for not reporting it to occupational health, it gave the guy a giant fig leaf to hide behind.

After the security man and Willie John had left, Bill summarised where he thought we were.

'This may be a cock and bull story, but his manager shouldn't have ignored him saying he felt faint on previous occasions, and you, Frank, shouldn't have said you knew he'd done it before. If you had asked something like *is this the first time*, he would probably have said "yes" and we would have him bang to rights for lying given the nurse's evidence of the bed being used multiple times.'

I interrupted, 'But...'

Then Willie John knocked on the door saying he needed to speak to Bill for a moment in private.

Bill returned a few moments later, looking glum.

Willie said the security man's going to get a low blood pressure certificate from his doctor about being prone to fainting and, if he's dismissed, they will be appealing in the strongest possible terms as he had mentioned his health issue to his manager.'

I erupted. 'It's all bollocks, we know he's been swinging the lead for ages, every time A shift is on, he's putting one over on us...'

'Probably, but you have the two weak spots in your case, it may be bollocks, but he now has possible excuses. In the light of this, I suggest the most he can get is a final written warning and three days' suspension for not formally reporting his illness and endangering the site.'

The security manager nodded his acceptance and I resignedly said, 'He's bloody well got off scot-free, sleeping on the job should be dismissal.'

'Well do it differently next time,' was Bill's tart reply.

We reconvened, and I could not fail to notice the smirk on the convenor's face. He knew I knew he knew, that I had been worked over.

I went back to the office to lick my wounds. I kicked the door shut, and the partition creaked. Anita looked in with raised eyebrows and I waved her away, making it clear I did not want to talk to anyone. Cockups happen, I said to myself but why did it have to be in front of an even newer personnel officer? I was staring into space when Bill came in. He sat down, thankfully not pulling out his cigarettes.

'Listen, just ask open questions in future, and don't give them the opportunity to create a case. At least you didn't mention the occupational health nurse had grassed him up.'

'I'm so bloody annoyed with myself and embarrassed for Tim as well, not exactly a great learning experience.'

'Forget it, the guy has probably learnt his lesson, as you and the manager have. We all win some and lose some in this job. Anyway, that's now history. Get over it, see you later.'

By now I had developed a headache, probably from the humiliation, so I walked briskly to the canteen, looking around to see if anyone was openly laughing at me. I would get a couple of pies, walk back lock my door with the blinds closed and seethe with rage.

'Hiya,' Anita caught up, almost jogging to keep up with the furious pace I was walking. 'You look really upset, what's wrong?'

'You do not want to know. Total cockup, I should be sacked.' She grabbed my arm, so I had to slow down.

'Wow, I'll buy you a pint after work if you like, you can cry on my new shoulder pads,' she said.

'I'm not sure what company I'll be, but thanks anyway.'

'Childe of Hale at six then,' she smiled and turned towards the press shop with disciplinary papers in her hand.

I had no time to feel sorry for myself back in the office, there was an industrial engineering work study report about the 'drillings' area on my desk. I brushed the crumbs from the cheese and onion pie off the report and skim read it. I had read three books a week in the local library as a youngster, I could read extremely fast by any standards. You didn't need to be an engineer to see that of the five men employed to drill holes for wing mirrors, reversing lights and the new rear fog lights, the utilisation was such that you could reduce the manning by one per shift. And they would still have spare time. It was on my desk because the line engineer knew the change in manning would be resisted and that it would end up with a labour dispute, ergo my job.

I brushed my second pie off the report and put my feet up on the desk. This was a great example of what the press called the 'British Disease.' I could envisage how it would go. The unions would not want to lose even one job per shift, but management needed these small productivity efficiencies to compete with the German plant. I rationalised both sides of the argument in my head; I could see with 2 million unemployed why unions were desperate to preserve jobs at any costs. I could also see that capitalism was international, the company would put future models where it got the best return. That was one thing Marx had got right. This was the third 'productivity enhancement' I'd handled in the short time I'd been there. There would be no agreement, management would impose it and the staff would walk out. Production would be lost and so some fudge brokered by personnel officers like me would happen. How good the local manager was and how militant the steward was might determine how good or bad the actual specific settlement was. Either way, the result would not be driven by the engineering science. It was a bloody farce.

Although I had been leftish at college, I knew firmly which side I was on in these disputes. I had ranted a bit to Willie

John and to other stewards about the huge number of these unofficial strikes, how they were killing the factories in the UK. The fact that the Fiesta city car had gone from Dagenham to Valencia made it so obvious. Before I had arrived, the Capri had already gone from Liverpool to Germany and the executive car was going too. Why could the unions not see the bigger picture, it was staring everyone in the face? I put the report down and picked up the 'Company Press Cuttings', produced by public relations upstairs in the office once a day.

I was shocked to see that Ford was going to invest $300 million in a Brazilian factory over the next three years. I was really surprised as I had read absolutely nothing about it before. British Leyland was in the press, as they were every single day. This time they were asking the UK government for another £500 million to ensure survival and were reported as wishing to axe 50,000 jobs. Then it was over the water to Vauxhall's who were on the fourth week of a strike, and whose unions were now blacking ports to prevent materials coming into the country. I shook my head in disbelief, I was not sure I could even get my head round the state of the industry. The politicians may have ceased to manage the country, but British management were also doing their best to cease managing the factories.

There was a knock on the door and the framing area Superintendent Charlie McManus came in with a general foreman, remaining standing. They were responsible for about 500 staff I reminded myself.

'Sorry to disturb your dinner, lad. Have you looked at the work study yet?'

'Yes, they'll love it,' I said, trying to be funny.

'You set up a meeting for us with engineering and the steward this afternoon and I'll try and get them to agree to an observational study as a way in.'

'Like the one on the rough discing where they just worked slow and messed about while being observed?' I said, in my normal straightforward way.

'Well, do you have a better idea?' said the superintendent.

'Yeah, sack them all and bring over 500 Turks from Germany,' I said jokingly.

'I'll drink to that,' he laughed, and they left.

I arranged the meeting in an office on the first floor of the factory, up some steel stairs overlooking the body side area. As I opened the door, the smoke wafted out; the others were already there. The sound of forklift trucks whirring, welding arc flashing and a little mechanical clicker recording each car as it came off the line greeted me. I wasn't late, but annoyingly they had started without me. What a way to make someone feel pissed off I thought. Lenny Lobo was in full flight.

'Youse average of seventeen vinyl roofs an hour means nottin' to us, because when they're all bunched together the lads can't cope,' his face as animated as a Hollywood actor. He continued,

'And I've heard there's a run out limited edition with a boot spoiler coming which requires six more drillings in the boot.' I looked at Charlie, as this was not in the work study report.

'We're expecting one or two an hour max, but until it's launched, we don't know what the take up will be,' said the engineer.

Lenny stood up, his face angry,

'We'll do the study when the limited edition is in, not before.'

'We want to start next Monday on days,' said Charlie.

'Norra chance, you can start the study after,' and Lenny got up and left.

Charlie turned slowly to the work study engineer and said,

'How the hell does the steward know of a limited edition before me? Just explain that.'

The engineer apologised profusely and said the limited edition had come out of some marketing guy's hat with no notice. He thought it would be another month yet, and that they could sort the new drillings manning before it hit the lines.

I was up to speed quickly. 'But if we introduced the new manning successfully and then had to put more people back in for the new edition a week or two later, they'd think we are idiots, surely?'

'Yes, but at least the new manning would then be in…'

Charlie cut across him.

'We've wasted two fuckin' hours on this, there is no chance of getting it in before this limited edition arrives, go and tell your boss that.' He got up, indicating the meeting was over.

The work study engineer left, I shrugged and clanked down the steel staircase, into the harsh lights of the body side assembly line, stopping halfway down to watch the drillers and rough discers at work. I had a childish fascination with the yellow sparks from the discs and the hiss of the compressed air on the drills. A car factory was a place where you could idle away hours if you were intrigued by the complexity of a roll of steel turning miraculously into a finished car. One of the lead discers spotted me staring and did a monkey gesture, like he was in a cage in a zoo being observed. I gave a mock salute and carried on down the stairs, walking slowly back to the piggeries thinking about the meeting, another disaster that good management would have avoided.

I had finished writing up the meeting notes when Anita knocked on the screen between our offices and pointed at her watch, I smiled and gave her the thumbs up. I packed up carefully, nothing could be left on desks without security writing a snotty report to your manager. Anita called in, with her trendy shoulder pads and gold earrings and we walked out together.

'How was your disciplinary?' I asked.

'It was a water bombing incident, so we decided on a final warning and one day's suspension,' said Anita.

'What, like horseplay then?' I said, never having heard of one before.

'Yes, just a childish prank gone wrong. The 1974 Health and Safety at Work Act's lost on the staff here.'

'Probably lost on me too,' I said.

We drove to the pub separately, only a couple of miles away but an oasis of calm set in the countryside and a real village. Anita arrived in her new silver Escort and me in my battered old Beetle. I felt I would love to just hold her and give her a lingering kiss, though I knew I would never in a million years have the nerve to do that.

I bought a pint of bitter and a lager and lime at the bar, and then sat down in the green snug area surrounded by old-fashioned wood and glass. We touched glasses.

'Cheers,' I said breathed out and settled into the softly upholstered bench, looking sideways, and noticing Anita's raised eyebrows.

'Oh, the big sister look is it then,' and laughed, leaning back for a good pull of the beer.

'I'm a good listener, just open your mouth and talk.'

I laughed again,

'You sound like Lauren Bacall, "Just put your lips together and blow."'

'Ok Rick, stop avoiding the question. I have heard about the sleeping case.'

'I'm sure the whole factory has by now,' I replied gloomily.

She sat there unmoving, waiting for me to speak. I looked sideways into her face, one which always seemed to have a half smile on it. She missed her vocation, she should have been a police investigator.

'It feels like the last straw for me. Every single day there are disputes, every single day we lose cars, no one seems to bloody well even care except me. You know, I lie there at night in my unheated flat, staring at the ceiling thinking what futile bullshit will happen the next day. I'm just getting sick of it… sorry, I said I wouldn't be much company.' Anita hooked her arm into mine, it was like an electrical shock. She twisted on the bench to look at me, her eyes sparkling.

'Just do another year and get industrial relations on your CV, there must be something better in the world of work than what we do here?'

'We're all doomed,' I said in a deliberate *Dad's Army* accent.

Anita laughed but still held my arm, I was liking her more and more. She turned slightly more towards me.

'I was walking up your production lines today, do you know anyone who would really, really want to do those tedious metal bashing jobs? Hour after hour, day after day, year after year? They'd drive any sane person to crave for industrial action just to stop the monotony.'

I thought affectionately of my own father, who had worked in a car factory since the war and my uncles likewise. Vauxhall, AC Delco, Bedford trucks. It was the only way of putting food on the table where they lived.

'My dad's done twenty years in a factory but at my age he was in the Atlantic on a Destroyer. It must have given him a different perspective on what a working life could be.'

'But he wouldn't have had your education or expectations, would he?'

'No… you're right. Sorry, I sound selfish, your family must have had it harder being hounded out by Idi Amin.'

'I hear the convenor got the better of you in the sleeping investigation?' she persisted.

I looked back at her,

'He did, I was properly humiliated, and he was laughing at me. Anyway, that was this morning I'm over it. I'll get the bastard back one day. Listen, kick me hard if I mention work one more time as I'm not going to sound like a bloody depressive all evening. So, umm what are you doing this weekend?'

Anita blinked at the sudden change in topic.

'Well, I usually go back to Leicester and see the family, it's a big thing with us Ugandan Asians.' She blushed, 'My mum is always arranging family dinners with doctors and engineers to marry me off,' and stared ahead waiting for my laugh. I looked directly at her, to see if she was joking and she turned to face me, slightly embarrassed.

'Seriously, like an arranged marriage then?' trying to keep a straight face. 'Well, if you don't go to Leicester we could go down to the docks, take in this new *Deer Hunter* film and maybe have lunch together.'

'I'll have to ask my mum.' My face fell, my mouth stopped as I was about to swallow a gulp of beer.

'Your face, I'm only kidding. That would be nice thanks.' She laughed and squeezed my hand.

I was beginning to like Anita even though she said her first view of me was that I seemed a bit serious, a bit intense, and overly aggressive on the state of the country and the shop stewards. She'd joined the company because it had a top reputation for its graduate scheme; I had joined to improve industrial relations in the car industry! She said she wasn't sure if I was naive or an idealist, but either way she kind of liked being treated like an equal, unlike with some of the older men.

When we left the pub, I was half considering kissing her, but I didn't have the nerve to. Maybe on Saturday. It was a date after all. I wondered what she would say to her mum, she wouldn't be happy that Anita wasn't going home this weekend.

Dispute

There was no room at the conference table for me, as one of the juniors, so I sat with the work study engineer on seats round the edge of the room. I wasn't that bothered, partly because Anita had agreed to another date and partly because I knew the meeting would be about the actual numbers for reduction. I listened as the superintendent, Charlie, explained how they had avoided industrial relations issues with the run out of the previous car model by not reducing labour. They were now 150% off the standard.

'To braze and rough disc now, we need a maximum of two men so we can remove two men per shift immediately.'

I sat forward. Remove four men per day… I'd yet to see the union concede that in my time at the plant. The site personnel manager Eric was present, so it must be important I thought.

'Local production and personnel will meet with the shop stewards and work study to agree the figures for this case. Management are determined to support this, so go away and do your jobs with that in mind.' I walked out with Bill, who said, 'If they'd bitten the bullet then, we wouldn't be having this discussion now, would we?'

'I can't see them agreeing to lose four jobs, whatever the boss says.'

I knew that the balance of two door, four door cars, estates and vans on the same line meant that work study was an inexact science. Then you had the arguments about changing disc pads, walking across the moving line and so on which always meant conflict. Anyway, the first step was an unofficial discussion with the shop steward and operators just to brief them on the plan and timings. I wandered out to listen to the conversation in the body in white area; there was no shouting, so I went back to the relative calm of my office. It was lunch time, Anita was not in her office, so I walked over to the canteen with Tim for lunch. Despite his background, Tim had settled in well. He was accepted as a genuine 'posh twat'; scousers liked authenticity and he was the real deal. His encyclopaedic knowledge of The Beatles also helped. We'd just sat down for pie and chips when the drillings area foreman rushed over to the table.

'They've gone home,' he paused, breathless.

'What do you mean, it's just exploratory talks?'

'They had a show of hands and all twenty-one just walked out.'

'For God's sake', I said. I wrapped up the pie in a napkin, left the chips and accompanied the foreman back to the BIW Superintendent's office. The production manager, Bill Ryman, the superintendent Charlie, Bill Budd, the general foreman, two shop stewards and the convenor were already there. Bill Ryman was in full cockney flow.

'We haven't even made a fuckin' proposal and they've walked out and stopped the fuckin' factory. What's the point in having a fuckin' procedure if they just bugger off eh? Do I lay off the nightshift eh?'

The convenor, Willie John butted in. 'Hold your horses. No one is saying the nightshift won't work normally.'

'You have one hour, or I'll be laying the nightshift off without pay. You know where I am.'

'I'll see the stewards in my office,' said Willie John and the meeting broke up. Their noisy Totectors boots rattled as they went down the metal stairs that led back to the factory floor. Bill Budd slumped down next to me with the Irish general foreman from the Dagenham factory.

'Is it the first time a strike has been called without the actual manning even being proposed?' I said through a mouthful of pie.

'It's a first even for me,' said Bill. 'I suspect they're getting their punches in first, or it's another inexperienced steward cockup.'

'That's what you get startin' a feckin factory with these lazy wankers, white heat of technology me arse, feck Harold Wilson,' said the general foreman. Bill and I looked at him open-mouthed. I bit my tongue for once. Dagenham was not as bad as Liverpool but was hardly an industrial relations nirvana.

Bill stood up.

'You two had better go and stop the pay of the twenty-one, hadn't you?'

I finished the pie as I walked back to the piggeries; you weren't supposed to eat food on the factory floor but sod it, I said to myself. All the lines were already stopped, though subassemblies were still working. Tim, Anita and Jim were camped out in my office, deadpan faces all round. I'd just sat down to explain when Bill poked his head round the door.

'Meeting in Eric's office in two minutes for a briefing on the walk out. Frank, you'll need to type up a stoppage report as soon as you can, number of men walking out, cars lost, you know the score.'

'Will do' I said, downhearted.' It wasn't my fault, but I still felt guilty that it was my personnel area that had shut down production yet again. We all trooped off to Eric's office.

Eric, sitting down with pipe in hand, spoke.

'I think you've all heard by now that A shift stopped due to a ridiculous unofficial strike in BIW.' His desk phone rang, someone else answered it and then his secretary buzzed through.

'That was Willie John, he's embarrassed enough to be coming in tonight to try and ensure B shift starts. Frank, you had better go home after this and be back for the nightshift start as well. Before you go, do you think it was a deliberate tactic on their part or an incapable junior steward?'

'Well, I've not spoken to Lenny yet but from the look on his face I would say it was the new steward as he's only been in the job five minutes,' I said.

'Ok. I hope that's the case.' He patted down his pipe, but thankfully didn't light the stinking thing.

'Everyone else needs to be in early tomorrow in case we're laying everyone off. I'll ring my opposite number in the PTA plant and Jim, you can ring Head Office to let them know the state of play.'

'I'll be as popular as a pig in a synagogue then,' laughed Jim.

'Thanks Jim, I know we can always rely on you for the humour.'

Driving home I reflected on the dispute. It felt like anarchy to me. The union could not control its members in these volatile situations. They never ever used the agreed disputes procedure. I smiled at my recent disagreement with Willie John, the union convenor, 'My members first, your employees second.'

My reply had been, 'Our employees first, your members second.'

We agreed to differ. Thatcher was on the car radio, talking about her new policy idea to have ballots before any strike action, rather than the current intimidatory show of hands. I thought about this current strike; for these unofficial or 'wildcat' strike situations ballots wouldn't make any difference at all. I wondered if the British really were too individual for roles that required conformity and doing exactly what you were told. The best car producing countries, like Germany and Japan, seemed to have a militarist history, although that was clearly an assertion with no evidence as my friend Pete would say.

At home, I went for a snooze as I was due back in a few hours and who knew what the night would bring and how long I would be there. As I lay on the bed and set my old mechanical alarm clock, I knew I would consider, for the first time in my relatively short life, voting for the Tories. How could I vote for Callaghan, Foot and Benn? Like Einstein said, if you keep doing the same things, you get the same results and the Labour Party had been doing that for at least six years.

At 10 p.m. Bill Ryman the shift manager, Charlie Murphy the superintendent, Bill and myself sat down in Ryman's factory floor office waiting to see if BIW started on time. Well, the shift never actually started on time; there was always some delay, something Herman the German had never sorted out and which riled him enormously. At 10-ish the line started and Willie joined us. He looked shattered.

'Well, the good news is B shift are working normally as ye can see. The bad news is a lot of new objections to the work study. Do you want to discuss them now or in the mornin'?' I would have preferred to hear them now, but Bill said we should meet at 10 a.m. in his office to have the benefit of the A shift views as well, and so we could also invite the work study engineers.

The effort of returning to work at night made me question whether I really had the patience for the grind involved in these miniscule improvements in productivity. Trying to prevent unofficial strikes and spontaneous walkouts was half of my current job. I may have no work or career alternative at the moment, but with so little success could I really be motivated to continue doing this in two years' time?

The next morning, A shift had started normally at six, so management were surprised by Willie John's startling announcement at the 10 a.m. meeting.

'I did nae come on the last banana boat up the Clyde. Your guarantees on car and van mix are nae worth the paper they are written on. We'll nae enter further discussions unless you guarantee to man up for the worst possible mix.'

I didn't know whether to laugh or admire their chutzpah. Even when Bill Ryman promised a gap in the line if line speed ever became unsustainable because of model mix, they refused further discussions. The meeting broke up in a stalemate.

On the way out, Willie John was quite aggressive, 'And if yon management try any kind of study with four men per shift less, they'll be an immediate downing of tools.'

The rest of that week, I spent most of the working day in interminable meetings with production management and work study. We often visited the lines on observations. The irony was that it was impossible to determine the practicality of the management proposal without trying it out. Some of the objections were technical, like how the van rear door complexity influenced line cycle times. There were meetings with health and safety about crossing the moving production line with dragging airlines. It was clear no one wanted to compromise, and each side had fixed positions. The usual car industry impasse. It frustrated me that the common good of making the factory competitive for future investment was never ever discussed, never seemed to be in anyone's mind but mine.

At the end of the week, following the intervention of the T and G district official and the IRM Eric, a 'check study' was agreed. This lasted just three job cycles before the two shop stewards disputed the timings and took thirty-three men off to a meeting, stopping production. The meeting cost thirty-two cars and the original manning was reverted to. I shrugged my shoulders and was in the office writing up the 'stoppage of work' report when the industrial engineer, Ken, who was working the job came in and sat down. He was bright, with a first from Imperial, London. I looked up at him and gurned, 'Well, you couldn't have tried any harder on this, they just don't want to move. I admire your will to keep at it.'

'Thanks. The reason I popped in was to hand in my resignation though, I'm joining Evans Medical just down the road.'

'What, just because of one dispute?'

'No, I decided to leave months ago; the job offer being today is just a coincidence. I feel I'm wasting my time here; no one disputes the science, but the unions have no interest in improving and management have no balls so I'm going somewhere with no unions.'

'Well after this week I know exactly how you feel. I've never been so frustrated in my life,' I said.

'If it doesn't work out, I did German at school so I might join the brain drain and go abroad. I'm too young to hang around to see if things ever change here.'

I nodded sympathetically, took the letter and agreed a leave date. We shook hands warmly. I couldn't help but think that if all the good guys left, those remaining would be the people who couldn't leave or were happy with the status quo. I tried to think positively about the future of the plant but however hard I tried, I just couldn't.

— 8 —

Deer Hunter

One cold afternoon, I had my first ever 'exit' interview. So many skilled tradesmen were leaving and emigrating that Personnel were being asked to try and find out why for a report to Head Office. My job was to interview a toolmaker who was emigrating to South Africa. He was in his late twenties, recently married and ambitious.

'I'm sick of the strikes and I can't afford the loss in pay. Honestly, I've been here three years post-apprenticeship and I can't see this factory being here in ten years. Even the *Sun* said we would soon be an 'offshore industrial slum' or something like that.'

'Why South Africa with its apartheid troubles, isn't that risky?' I said.

'Nah, we visited my brother out there this summer, big house, two cars, maid, and inflation is less than half it is here. Also, there's no closed shop crap. That's the future for me.'

'Some of the electricians we've seen are going to Canada or Australia, did you consider that?'

'Yeah, looked at Australia and we have the points to get in; my wife's a nurse and they're in short supply too. But my brother is in Durban, so we're going there.' He handed over his resignation letter and I just wished him all the best.

A toolmaker and two electricians all in the same week was worrying. It wasn't just the graduate 'brain drain' of scientists that the newspapers were full of, it was the shortage of skilled tradesman that were now causing production issues. I wrote up the proforma report and posted it to the personnel manager in the internal mail.

It was snowing again when I drove to the scrapyard to get a new regulator. The car had the engine over the drive wheels in the back so traction should have been good, but it was compromised by the cheap cross-ply remould tyres I had on. I made a mental note to get four decent tyres later that week. There were various local authority disputes going on and no gritting lorries at all; it was turning into dire winter, not just weather-wise, but also the continuous strikes breaking out everywhere. No wonder South Africa and Australia seemed so attractive. At least Anita had confirmed a Sunday cinema visit was on with a new gimmicky 'Post-it' sticky on my desk – so it wasn't all gloom and doom.

The journey to the Cunard building was littered with street rubbish and a foggy halo hung over the mean streets of the city of Liverpool. I cheered myself up by thinking that at least, there were no power outages and three-day weeks, and no 50 mph speed limits to conserve petrol. I made a mental note not to get into discussing 'politics' with Anita. I'd noticed her looking glassy eyed the last time I went off on one, I would save that for the stewards and my friend Pete. I parked up near the Three Graces and put on my old Crombie coat before I went to meet Anita at the Pier Head. I was surprised how much taller she looked in the wedge-shaped black boots she'd on and with her black bob and big white gold earrings she looked stunning. I was determined to be brave and hooked my arm in hers after a peck on the cheek and whirled her round towards the town.

'Come on, let's get moving before we freeze to death! I'd forgotten how cold the river wind is here.' We both chuckled and walked along the almost derelict dock front, over the road and vaguely towards Lime street station. I had left my A–Z of Liverpool in the car and had to keep stopping to look around, the soft snow made it difficult but after finding St George's Hall I was there. I glanced at Anita as we walked gingerly along, arm in arm.

'Shall we get a real filter coffee in the theatre, make a change from that stuff we drink so much of?' she said smiling.

'Great, you grab that table and I'll get them in,' I said. I admired the old Victorian decor, the couples chatting away in the usual animated Liverpool way. I returned and sat beside her on the leather bench type seat. I noticed again, her semi-permanent smile, it wasn't affected it just seemed to be always there.

'What are you laughing at?' she said.

'Oh nothing, just being with you seems to make me feel good,' regretting it as soon as I'd said it, it came out sounding cheesy.

'Sycophant,' was her slightly barbed response.

'Lovely coffee with the warm milk on top as well, really nice,' I said.

'Are you ok with seeing *The Deer Hunter,* it's got Robert de Niro and a new actress called Meryl Streep in it.'

'Oh yes, the *Guardian* gives it five stars.'

'You read the *Guardian?*' I said, in a surprised tone, spilling my coffee. Isn't it all public sector and academic stuff these days? I've landed on the *Times* and the *Sun*.'

The *Sun*, she looked at me incredulously. 'What for, the Page 3?'

I sounded more defensive than I meant to – 'I want to know what the man on the Clapham omnibus is thinking not some trendy new leftie in Camden market.'

We got up to go and I said quietly, 'Thanks for coming out with me, it's been such a shit week at work.' We walked up to the Odeon, I grabbed her arm when she went backwards down a kerb, and although she gave me an old-fashioned look, she didn't take it away again. The cinema had a huge screen, utterly amazing sound quality for the haunting theme tune, and for the powerful film sets. When the lights went up, I looked at Anita and she'd tears in her eyes. She was not embarrassed as I would have been, she just took out a tissue and wiped them.

'That took my breath away, what a film,' she said.

'I agree. That's up there with *Lawrence of Arabia* for me, absolutely bloody brilliant. If that's the Vietnam War. Phew.'

We watched all the screen credits and listened again to the music, most people had shuffled out when we rose to go. We walked out and I felt we seemed to have passed some criteria for a decent first date.

'Any preference for type of food?' I asked.

'As long as it's not Indian, I'm easy.'

'Well, you may be an expert on Asian cuisine, I'm an expert on pie and chips, lucky for you there won't be any of those round here.' We walked back towards the cars and Anita said there had been a review in the *Liverpool Echo* of a new restaurant overlooking the docks.

'Great, let's see if they still have views of dead dogs and old prams from the windows then,' and we walked along to the restaurant. I didn't have a positive feeling about the place as there was only one other couple. It smelt damp with electric fan heaters and condensation streaming down the windows. It was too far to walk back to town to find anywhere else, so we were stuck.

We took seats by the window but did not take off our coats. We chatted for a while and then I plucked up the courage to ask,

'Would you like to go out again sometime?'

'Maybe,' she said

'Oh.'

'Sorry, I meant to say I really enjoyed today but it's kind of complicated.'

I waited expectedly. She sat forward. 'Well, you're a work colleague and we've both seen in our office how work relationships can be complicated and I'm probably going to leave the factory if not the company soon.'

I sat saying nothing, shocked.

'Frank, have you ever met any Asians before, did you go to school with any?'

'Not sure why that's relevant but no, no one in my school I can recall.'

'Well, I have quite a claustrophobic set of relatives, always telling what to do and who to see. I'm not joking when I say my mum would expect me to be chaperoned today.'

'Seriously?' I said.

'I have also put up with nearly two years of leering, patronising managers and stewards just to prove to myself I can hack it. But for what, I'm not sure I want to stay in personnel management, half of the job is endless problem solving and half of it trivial. My college friends are in banks and consultancies working hard but on triple the salary advising on change and business consultancy.'

'But if we make even a small difference in improving industrial relations in a factory of this size and importance…'

'But Frank, the last fifteen years of poisonous Dagenham managers coming up here telling people how it's done better down south makes it impossible to make progress. When you add in the radical unions it could be an MBA thesis for a failing plant.'

'Well, I didn't know you felt that way,' I muttered.

The food arrived and was actually good, but we ate it almost in silence with Anita's speech like an elephant hanging over us. I knew I wasn't imagining it when we left, as it was back to a peck on the cheek and 'See you Monday.'

As I drove back towards Gateacre, I knew I was pleased to have asked her out as it was a lovely day, until the meal. I was debating with myself if I should've asked her if I'd done something to upset her, but I knew I was totally crap at understanding the moods of women. I was learning at work that being direct seemed to get me into all sorts of trouble, with women it seemed even worse. I might ask her if she'd enjoyed it on Monday, but then again it might be better to see if she raised it first. I had really liked her company and would love to go out again but given what she had said about her circumstances that now didn't seem likely.

Porn

I had arrived early on the Monday just in case I could casually bump into Anita to hear what she was thinking about Saturday, when Jim popped his head round the door,

'Bill wants to see us right now, he's got a job for us with a bit of overtime I'm thinking,' rubbing his hands.

Bill was sitting in his smart office doing paperwork; he looked up as we went in.

'Ok, there's a strange job for you two this Friday night, and you might need to take Tim, although he's a bit short of experience for this.'

'What?' I said suspiciously.

'Last Friday night, the fire sprinklers went off over the body side storage area in framing, rusting the steel and causing a right mess. The fire engineer who investigated it said the sprinklers were deployed because of a build-up of heat in the plant room above the area. He went up there and found a Super 8 projector and a load of chairs.' Jim and Bill looked at me to see if I could guess where this was heading.

'And?'

Jim butted in,

'There's a load of operators welt working, crammed into the plant room watching porn films and it's setting off the bloody sprinklers below!'

'Yes, right. Ok, what's the foreman doing then?' I said.

'We believe he was up there with them,' said Bill frowning. 'So, I want you two and the general foreman to be in on nights and surprise them, with Tim on the other exit door in case anyone tries to leg it.'

'I'd prefer Anita, Tim's a bit laid back and colonial for this,' I said.

'I am not having any woman back on nights on the factory taking names at a porn show. End of. They might all charge for the doors when you put the lights on.'

'It's alright if we get pushed down the stairs then is it?' I said.

'I can't see anyone pushing a big bugger like you down the stairs,' said Jim snidely.

'Look, if there's a need for a fourth person I'll do it, but then I can't hear any appeals so let's organise without me if possible,' said Bill.

I thought for a moment, 'What exactly is the offence then?'

'Yes, I'm thinking about that. At least leaving the place of work without permission.'

'And if the foreman gave permission?' I said.

'Could be dismissal for the foreman, written warning for the punters, but could be dismissal for some under totting up procedure anyway,' said Bill.

'So, original question, what exactly is the offence?' I said again.

'Ok, ok, yes we'll have to think about that. Right, the plant office is Jim's area really, but the operators are yours. Jim, you brief Tim. Isn't Tim a black belt in kung fu or something?' laughed Bill.

We broke up and went our separate ways. Whatever you think about personnel work, it is sometimes exciting.

The news came through during the day that the huge UK public sector unions were calling a national strike which was for 1.5 million workers! It was covering hospitals and ambulances, alongside the recently announced twenty-four-hour train staff disputes. I was apoplectic at the local news as well. In Liverpool, the gravediggers were asking for a 46% wage increase when inflation had probably come down from around 30% to nearer 10%. A factory in Liverpool had already been rented for the storage of corpses. You couldn't make it up, it was a total disaster.

I realised that although I had seen Anita a couple of times in the distance that week, when she was in the office, she seemed to have a continual stream of meetings. Anyway, my planning for the Friday night porn show and my own area's disputes and disciplinaries kept my mind on the job in hand. Friday afternoon involved a planning meeting in Bill's office, and I turned up early for once. I looked jealously out of the large window over the car park, with the Speke council housing estate in the distant background. The weather was still cold, but there was a watery blue sky with dark clouds high up, running fast. I was still gazing out when the others showed up and Bill called the meeting to order.

'I've just agreed with Eric, I'm now going to be in the security lodge tonight as we don't trust security not to ring ahead. Also, Tim has a complete list of all the nightshift framers, and he can check them off. If they give a false name, they will need to know the employee number too, which is highly unlikely. The plan is for you three to sneak into the factory and up the outside stairs with Charlie the superintendent, turn on the lights and nobble them all. If the foreman is there you can suspend him but send the others back to work and we'll hold disciplinaries on Monday morning, as shift changes over then anyway.'

'There goes a missed overtime opportunity,' said Jim.

'Just remember this is an absolute first for personnel to plan something like this, so let's be careful how it goes. See you all later.'

We all left at 3 p.m. to be back in for 2 a.m. Anita had not been there again but I remembered she'd been out on a Kepner-Tregoe course for two days, whatever that was.

Jim picked me up at 1.30 a.m. in his new grey Cortina, Tim was in the front. I couldn't help but think about the recent Tom Robinson band song of the same name… and hummed 'Wish I had a grey Cortina'. I noticed it had XL badges but

Ghia trim alloy wheels and Ghia trim velour seats. Jim noticed me looking at the car.

'Had to pay a steward to fix it like, paid a few quid for some extra bits to be substituted like' and he smirked into the mirror.

'I thought that list they stuck to the bonnet of cars these days made sure the right bits were fitted?'

'With so many stoppages the paper sometimes conveniently falls off, as long as the bits can be ordered as an option for the model it's no problem if you grease a few palms. They'll notice when they audit but just think it's a cockup with those Bangladeshis they employ down there who can't read English and put stuff on according to coloured stickers.'

'Bloody hell Jim if there's a scam you're in on it.' We turned into the security lodge and saw through the half-light there that Bill was raising the barrier, presumably ensuring no one could page or ring ahead that three personnel officers were back on nights. Charlie, the Scottish superintendent, was sitting in the dark, waiting for us in Jim's office.

'Right lads, we're going the back way so we should be able to get to the plant room door without the vagabonds seeing us.' I could smell the tension in the room, I hoped it went better than the sleeper in the nurse's bed cockup I'd been involved with.

'Aye, let's away,' said Charlie and we trooped out surreptitiously like it was a wartime commando raid.

We walked quickly into the harsh fluorescent light; Tim was the only one carrying a clipboard. I liked the tension of it all. It was certainly going to be material for at least a good joke. As we got near to the plant room, Tim went round the back to the emergency fire escape and started to quietly climb it. The rest of us were now emerging into public view at the bottom of the main plant room stairs. We were finally noticed by the line operators who started shouting 'Spies, spies, spies' as we began to climb the metal staircase. I laughed. I couldn't see how anyone would hear them given the volume of the film as we reached the door.

Charlie waited till we were together on the platform, opened the door and reached inside to turn on the lights,

'Aye, aye lads, what's this then, a porn film?' Someone turned off the projector, a shout went up and chairs clattered over as they started to stand up. Those nearest the fire escape tried to rush the fire door to find it locked shut. The small room stank from the sweaty operators.

'Ok lads, the games up, you can file out this way giving your name and number,' as Tim eventually opened the fire escape door and joined the party. I noticed the embarrassed foreman, skulking behind a particularly fat operator.

'Don't tell me, all eight of you are on a relief break,' said Jim jokingly.

'Dat's right, we've all got ring burn from a bad curry. Fair cop like…'

Charlie said to the foreman that he would see him in his office in five minutes. He looked at Tim. 'Who gave you the key to lock the door?'

'I didn't, I wedged it,' and took out of his pocket an old grey rubber door wedge.

'What would you have done if there had been a fire?'

'Removed it,' said Tim.

'Jesus, you've got a lot to learn about Health and Safety laddie,' said Charlie.

Tim took the names and numbers of the eight men involved as they all returned sheepishly to the lines down below. Job done.

As we walked down the stairs, we were greeted with whistles and shouts of 'Narks, narks, narks' from the operators still working. Jim gave them his customary V sign. The superintendent went to meet the foreman to suspend him for serious misconduct, pending a hearing on Monday. Tim, Jim and I went to pick up Bill from the lodge and brief him about the evening events. We went to Bill's office where he unlocked a cabinet and produced four whiskey tumblers and a half bottle of malt. I was surprised as I knew alcohol was banned in all offices but joined in as we laughed loudly at the evening's events and eventually shook hands on how well it had gone. I then said on a serious note, 'How slack is the manning if eight of them can be off the job at once? No wonder the quality is so bad on nights; it's a bloody disgrace we allow it.'

'Welcome to the world of welt working,' said Bill.

'Did you see the kipper on that foreman,' said Jim. 'I'll be dining out on that for years to come, and eight hours' overtime. Legend, mates, legend.'

Bill dismissed us and Jim, still animated, prattled on all the way to dropping me off at my flat.

— 10 —

Welt

The next day, as I carried my car battery down the outside stairs from the flat to the car park, I made a mental note to get to the scrapyard for a new regulator, though now that I was working why not just get one from a VW dealer? Old habits die hard. Scrapyard.

There were no lights on in the four piggeries offices, so I guessed I was first in. I looked at my diary and saw three disciplinary meetings scheduled, so just another day at the office. At least there were welding flashes inside the factory, so they must be producing cars.

The first hearing was simple, a brazer admitted being absent from his place of work for the second time with no excuse. I wrote out a first written warning using a template letter, within three minutes of the steward and foreman leaving the office, and as there was no peep from the union steward about it I guess he thought they must have got off lightly.

The second one was slightly more complex, as it involved a CO2 welder downing tools while his grievance about welding splashes getting through his protective clothing was being discussed. The relief man had covered the job, no cars were lost and a written warning was given again with no fuss from the steward, who was narked by the incident because the welder had stopped work without even telling the steward.

The third was a returner from sickness absence, it was his fourth absence now in three months and there were always different reasons for the absence. I was clear in my mind the guy was skiving off, but I reluctantly agreed a review period. No improvement would mean a frustration of contract termination. The nightshift steward seemed anxious to get home, no special pleading was made, and we were finished by eleven.

I was writing up the last disciplinary letter and looked to see if Anita was there for a coffee, but she must have been out in the factory somewhere. A knock on the door revealed Johnnie Murphy, the Welfare PO. He was in his usual old barathea blazer and had the *Racing Post* under his arm. The rumour was that there were enough death-in-service widows to see, sick people to visit and funerals to go to, to keep him fully occupied. I did not have much respect for him; if there was a contentious job, he just made himself scarce.

'Err, I've gorra spare ticket for the dogs on Saturday night, if yer interested like? It comes with chicken and chips or scampi and chips.'

'In a basket?' I said.

'Have you bin before then?'

'No, just guessed how it would be. Sorry, but I'm going out with a mate to the flicks so no can do.' He looked crestfallen. As he left, Charlie, the framing superintendent, put his head round the door.

'Yuh can forget the drillings work study, there's been a surge of orders for metallic paint cars with vinyl roofs and that rubber spoiler on the boot. I'll have a wee look when the limited edition is over, until then we'll no instigate the change.' He shook his head in disgust, shut the door, and left. I stroked my chin while thinking and made a diary note for the next time I was on subs on nights, to see if two workers were actually using the jigs and doing the drillings or whether they were working one on and one off, which I suspected.

That afternoon Eric Moore, the personnel boss, had called a special meeting for us labour relations officers. Everybody had been out in the factory in the morning, so he met us at 2 p.m. in the afternoon. We were gathered in his smart office, loads of natural light and easily big enough for a meeting of seven of us.

It was where I had been on my first day in the factory when the nine-week strike had started.

Eric put his pipe down and looked round the room at the five labour relations officers; Bill and the white-collar personnel manager were there too. Eric always talked without notes like he was a barrister and in an accent that sounded like Harold Wilson's.

'I want to talk to you about "welt working".' I knew what it was, it was a local Liverpool word that originated from the Port of Liverpool Dockers.

'You all know that running the production lines without tea breaks requires the company to supply "relief men". The one to eight ratio was designed to allow a man two twenty-minute breaks. However, we have approximately 15 to 20% overmanning, which coupled with men also working back up the line, leads to poor quality work and the worst right-first-time performance in Europe.' I listened intently wondering what we would be asked to do.

'Halewood Body and Assembly Plants are infamous for operators not working to process, not doing jobs properly, mostly to create more personal time off the job. In some cases, operators are working two on, one off, half an hour about.' He picked up his pipe and tapped it on his ashtray.

'Remedial work to the cars because of the consequent quality issues means that the lines have to run 20% slower than they should be. This is creating a vicious circle of overtime to keep up with sales, which the operators naturally like, and ramps up our cost per car even further. So, from a date to be agreed, all sections will take out excess headcount and use official work study standards and any supervisor condoning welt working will be subject to disciplinary action.'

There was a collective intake of breath (I now realised why the white-collar staff personnel guy was present).

'You are also expected to crack down hard on any late arrivals and early leavers, we want the lines starting and finishing on the button. Any questions?'

He tapped on his pipe and began to fill it from a pouch of St Bruno. No one uttered a word, all thinking what this would mean for industrial relations and their day-to-day jobs.

Jim was the first to speak,

'I take it we don't need the cars like, 'cos this means war.'

Eric looked over his reading glasses like an academic. 'Jim, we're supposed to produce 836 cars a day, we lose on average about 100 cars a day to disputes, poor quality and welt working. Robotics innovations mean the capital required for the new model has gone up dramatically, so it's even more expensive than usual. There are only two plants in Europe that the new model is going to; if we're not one of them it's a slow death anyway.'

I put my hand up and quickly put it down again realising I was no longer at school. 'If Jim is right and we do lose cars in the short term with this issue, will the hopeful increase in productivity still mean we have a chance at the new model?'

Eric took off his glasses. 'I believe so yes, but if we don't do this, inside these four walls, I doubt if we have a future at all. Not as part of this company anyway. Frank, you've reminded me of something. Bill, we need to stop all recruitment from next week, we can use the redeployed staff from enforcing the proper manning to handle natural turnover. One other thing, our quality and strike record means our German friend upstairs is not necessarily supporting that the new model comes here anyway. We really must try and change that.'

I couldn't resist commenting even though I knew I shouldn't. 'I'll be unpopular for saying this, but if I was the chairman and it was my money, I'm not sure I'd invest it here.' There was a negative murmur from the others. 'Half the stewards don't seem to care if the factory is successful, they see profit as unpaid wages and the other half want to see it nationalised for Christ's sake.' Anita leant over and said 'Hear, hear' in my ear.

Eric looked directly at me, unsmiling.

'That's as it may be, but your job is to reduce their influence and help turn the factory round before it's too late. It's worth saying that the international news on the state of the country with transport strikes, public service pickets and the like is also unsettling our American shareholders.'

The meeting broke up. On the walk back to the piggeries Jim rubbed his hands together.

'Cheer up lads, this is a serious overtime opportunity, we'll soon be in here sacking people on twelve-hour nights. Unless management bottle out, cos I've seen that before.'

That night, I had been eating a takeout Chinese in front of my portable black and white TV. *Dallas* was on, I soon became tired of the backstabbing Ewings and wondered if that really was capitalism at its crassest or was essentially the same as where I worked? As I turned it off in disgust the phone rang. It was the drillings foreman from work. Five drillers had walked out, stopping production completely. He was ringing me because it was in my area. After I got off the phone, I remembered that they hadn't implemented the new standards yet, so was it really because of the vinyl roof rear aerofoil complication? Why had I not asked the foreman that on the phone? I knew that the one key thing to decide was whether this was an 'unconstitutional stoppage of work' by a group of employees or an 'individual disciplinary issue' for five employees? Shit, well I would have to work it out in the morning as there was nothing I could do now. If it was the latter, the offence could be either 'refusing a reasonable instruction' or maybe 'unauthorised absence'. Maybe even 'leaving the place of work without permission' I thought. But if it was the five operators all at once, it must be an unconstitutional stoppage with no disciplinary action. I drifted back to sleep on the floor mattress.

I made the short drive into work next day with a heavy heart. It always puzzled me that disciplinary meetings on shift in working time happened in the production offices out on the factory floor, but if operators were called back in the next day they were always in the personnel offices, not that my office could accommodate five operators anyway.

I had never before asked the personnel office handyman, known colloquially as a 'gofer' in Liverpool, to do anything. Today I had found him in his cleaning cupboard reading horse form. I asked him (he was known as 'Soft Mick'), to put a jug of water with some glasses in one of the conference rooms before the hearings started. I was reluctant to use his services because I had never had a proper explanation of why he was on the personnel office headcount. I thought back to the ridiculous conversation I'd had with Jim a couple of months ago.

'You are saying we have a full-time employee as a "gofer" on our personnel headcount?'

'Well, he's not just a "gofer", he's also the "can lad".'

'What's that mean?'

'Well, like, if you ask him to get you a bacon butty or take a message somewhere he will. If he likes you. He's just a bit slow, and he's always hiding.'

'Why can't we get our own bacon butties?'

'Because then he'd have nothing to do,' said Jim.

I had assumed from his name that he must be mentally disabled and Irish. It turned out he was neither, no one claimed to know his real name anymore and he'd had a mini-stroke a few years previously.

'We're just keeping him on for a few years till he's eligible for his pension, his wife died and he's no kids, so this is home,' Jim had explained.

'That's his full-time job?' I asked incredulously. Jim laughed,

'Well, if you see the speed he walks at that's it, apart from taking racing bets.'

When I had first met him, he was actually in what looked like a wartime demob suit. It was held up with a cloth belt round the waist, he was now so gaunt he must have lost a lot of weight since the war. Part of his face did not move at all. His stock response to any request was always,

'Ah've just sat down,' as he was reluctant to do anything. An hour later, he just managed to get the water and glasses into the meeting room. He was wiping up the spillages from his shaky hands, as I walked in.

'M-M-Mr Thomas must be time for me brek now?' doffing a make-believe hat.

'Ok Mick.'

I shook my head after Mick had left. I still did not know whether it was completely ridiculous or extremely charitable. It confirmed my view that you could never understand Liverpudlians unless you grew up there; anyone thinking anything else was deluded.

The loss of a whole night's production meant the meeting would be chaired by Bill Ryman, the A shift manager, with Charlie Murphy, the framing area superintendent. Bill Budd and myself would join the meeting too. Before anyone arrived, I lay back in the soft leather chair looking at the ceiling and waiting for the others. At least B shift was working normally. The mood was glum, as they all filed in to join me, and John Benny, a newish steward, shuffled in as well. I knew the walk out could not be about the work study on vinyl roofs and boot spoilers but was still surprised to hear it was a straightforward difference of opinion on the current model mix manning. Charlie relayed the issue: the short-term mix of vans to three and five door cars meant they temporarily needed fewer people. The supervisor redeployed them and they had refused to work.

Bill Ryman listened for once. He looked at the steward and said, 'So, you didn't bother putting it into the disputes procedure and raising a grievance, you just let them leave?' He didn't wait for a reply from the steward. 'I really have heard it all now, 400 cars, 400 cars for Christ's sake.' The steward finally got an angry word in.

'I didn't know this was coming. I was away elsewhere stopping a dispute with the rough discers, I didn't know you were taking a man off the job did I? By the time I got there, they'd all pissed off home.' The steward then stood up left the meeting.

Ryman looked at Charlie, Bill Budd and me and said, 'I want the two of you to find a way of sacking the five fuckers asap. Just tell me how you're going to do it by tomorrow night.'

I looked at Bill for support, but he just sat there pondering what Ryman had said. I responded, as I always did and always knew I shouldn't.

'For what? If it's unofficial action, sacking them will be seen as victimisation. If it's an individual misconduct, walking off the job is hardly serious misconduct and not sackable anyway.'

Ryman looked like he would explode, his face red as a beetroot.

'Four hundred cars is as fuckin' serious as it gets, just find a way.' He got up and slammed out, followed by Charlie looking pensive. After they had gone, Bill said, 'Frank just let him blow, you're winding him up arguing like that. He'll calm down. Just write down a few points about the risks of doing what he suggests and talk to him later. Don't argue face to face with him like that when he's clearly emotional. By the way, we didn't lose that many cars last night.'

I looked at him puzzled, 'How can that be, the shift never got…'

'He must have had a stash somewhere' and laughed. It had been long rumoured that the sister plant in Germany had a stash of hidden cars, so if there were technical difficulties, they would still produce the schedule on the button. Maybe Bill Ryman really was the crafty cockney and was taking a leaf out of their book.

Bill suggested I went home and came back in for the start of the A shift at ten that evening, which I reluctantly did. I looked for Anita for a chat before I left, but she was out in the factory again.

Driving home, the radio news was full of the Jim Callaghan 'Crisis, what Crisis?' statement, after he'd been filmed stepping off an aeroplane from the Caribbean with a suntan. The 17% Ford workers had been paid had influenced a petrol tanker driver dispute so there were now miles of queues at petrol stations. With the lorry drivers still striking there were food shortages appearing. Worse for me, although the T and G and GMB unions were organised on a production plant basis, the skilled unions were organised geographically on a regional basis across industries. Their factory fitters, electricians and toolmakers could be influenced by the threatened national skilled unions strike action. I was not sure, I really needed to find out. I had still not got my head round the politics.

I reheated a couple of Cornish pasties I had bought in the local corner store and turned on the old TV for the news. Len Murray, the TUC leader and Moss Evans the T and G leader were headline news with anti-government pay policy messages, and an unprecedented public sector pay strike was looming. I decided to get some kip as the nightshift could be a long one, drifting off listening to the sound of chaos.

I went back in for the start of the 10 p.m. shift and was amazed to see old-fashioned military ambulances on duty, like something out of a wartime film. They didn't seem able to travel above 25 mph and were clearly to do with the ambulance men's strike. They were like the Green Goddess military fire engines used in the previous firemen's strike. I shouted out loud in frustration, the country looked like it was being run by Basil bloody Fawlty.

I waited in the production offices where I could overlook the lines, but Charlie the superintendent was surprised to see me.

'Did ye not hear? There's a big meeting tomorrow morning with the IRM and plant manager, so they have promised to work normally tonight.'

For God's sake, I thought, why had Bill not rung me to let me know? I checked they were indeed working normally and walked out to drive home, it was freezing cold. A complete waste of an afternoon and evening. Another company classic.

I was looking forward to the meeting the next day, I had no dealings with the overall body plant manager, a Harry Wolfson, ex-Dagenham plant and highly rated by reputation. The IRM Eric would be there, so it would be fascinating to see if there was a calibre difference between them and the middle management that I had dealt with to date. There was no doubt some of the street wise stewards could out manoeuvre the foreman and general foreman, and the middle managers often just shot themselves in the foot, by not thinking things through. I wasn't sure whether this was because the jobs were demanding and they had no time to think, or just their lack of intellectual horsepower. How could dismissing five drillings operators not lead to a full dispute? Unless the company literally did not want to produce cars and wanted to save wages, how could it be good management practice? And if they pushed it until they had to back off, management would lose even more credibility. But what did I know, given the short time I had actually spent here? Sometimes I felt I was on a different planet.

The meeting was in the plant manager's office, a huge office with a large oak table. It could seat at least twenty-five people, but we were down one end of it. I wondered how this could even be in the same building as my piggeries' office. Each place setting had a green leather blotting pad. Water, tea, and biscuits were brought in by an actual tea lady in a uniform, no shitty Klix here. The office was an oasis of calm and tranquillity, apart from the click click click of a mechanical car counter, as bodies left the plant and made their way to the paint shop in the next-door PTA plant.

Harry Wolfson was short, fit looking with Jewish features. He was obviously clever, educated and an East End cockney. Eric, the ultimate personnel boss on site, Bill Ryman, Charlie Murphy, Bill Budd and I were there. (I realised I was lucky to be invited, I normally got cut out of meetings at this level as too junior.) After introductions, I was surprised to see almost no discussion. Wolfson just summarised the issue and then eyeballed each of us in turn and asked us to give our personal view on his question, 'If we dismiss the five drillers, what is the percentage chance of the rest of the body in white section walking out in sympathy?'

Bill Ryman replied first. 'Twenty five per cent max and it's worth the risk to teach them a lesson about unconstitutional action.'

Bill Budd was next. 'Forty per cent as they have always supported each other in disputes in framing in the past.'

Charlie then said, 'Thirty per cent only, the door hangers and discers are pissed off with the drillers just downing tools and walking out without a by your leave.'

Wolfson obviously skipped Eric and went next to me. 'Ninety five percent, ok ninety. In the shortish time I've been here, not once has the company not caved in on a walkout, why is this any different? They know that.' There was a short pause while Wolfson stared at me.

'Thank you, gentlemen.' He paused for effect like some kind of actor. 'Eric and I have privately concluded even 10% is too high, when we are 4000 cars behind schedule, and we know we'll lose cars when we crunch welt working. Your figures confirm that, and we need the cars.'

Bill Ryman started to protest, but he was cut off by Eric, 'Harry and I have already called this, it's better they don't go out at all, than they go and we have no way of getting them back without losing face. We are saving our ammo for the welt working crunch.'

We looked at each other then silently trooped out, without even time to finish the tea and biscuits, the whole meeting was ten minutes maximum. Bill Ryman and Charlie Murphy walked off to the production offices while Bill and I wandered back down to the personnel offices, each lost in our own thoughts. Bill said, 'Try for first written warnings, with the five drillers, ok? We must desperately need the cars to allow them to get away with that.' We reached the bottom of the stairs.

'One other thing. With Bill and Charlie saying 25% did you really have to say 90%? You need a bit more nous, you might have thought more about the impact and said say 60%. They'll see it that you've embarrassed them in front of the boss. Don't reply, just think on it.'

I frowned and carried on to my office. I had always said what I had thought was right and took pride in being straightforward, but it was definitely doing me no favours in this job. It was another ticking off from the boss. I was brassed off and l agonised over whether saying 50% or 60% would really have made any difference. I didn't think so.

— 11 —

Sick pad

One afternoon the following week I looked at my wall clock, I needed to be going as I was back in at ten o'clock that night for 'subs' though I was not sure who else was on shift with me. This meant coming back to the factory on nightshift on payday and deciding who could have an advance on wages because they had financial issues. It was normally overdue gas bills, rent and so on. I still thought it a Victorian practice encouraging fecklessness, incredibly old-fashioned and archaic but nobody listened to me.

I was getting up to leave when Bill came in, unlit fag on his lips, and sat down rather than standing at the door. He stroked his moustache, 'Hey Frank, just wanted to catch you before you left for subs tonight. Anita has requested she be allowed to do subs night, so she's coming in with you tonight for the first time.'

'Really?'

'I'm not happy with a woman in here on nights, a lone worker in these shit offices next to 5000 men. Eric has overruled me, says she has to show she can do the whole job, equality and so on.'

'It's hardly the most difficult part of the job, is it…' Then I laughed, given my own first experience of causing a walk out doing subs. Bill got the reference, frowned and got up to go.

'Seriously, don't let her out of your sight. Ok?'

'Of course.' I was pleased, it was right that the slightly patronising sexist attitude should change, but I would keep an eye on her all the same. I had heard that a personnel officer refusing a sub was threatened with a knife a few years ago. I waited for five minutes in case Anita came back to her office but she didn't, so I left a post-it on her desk saying I would see her that night for a coffee before we opened for punters at 10 p.m.

On the drive home I heard the general situation in the country had deteriorated yet again. The 5 p.m. news on the radio was full of the health care workers' strike. A government minister had been blacked from receiving cancer treatment in hospital, as it was being rationed by the union stewards. Union stewards were deciding which kids were having lifesaving cancer treatment according to the more lurid press, it was causing outrage among the general population. I was shocked, it was like the Russian Revolution when the Bolsheviks decided who was treated and who was not. If you were seen as bourgeois, aristocratic or a shopkeeper you just died.

The bin men's strike had got worse, the pictures of the bins overflowing in Leicester Square six feet high and the size of the rats was humiliating for the country. At least the petrol tanker drivers had called off their pay dispute so I could fill up without queuing for the first time for ages. Jesus Christ... how bad could this get? I drove in and looked at the overflowing bins outside the flat. We had already lost two car spaces to the extra rubbish and the stench and hygiene was becoming a serious hazard.

I was going to ring Anita and suggest sharing a lift into work, as she'd have to drive past my flat to get there. I did think about inviting her for a drink before we started, but it wasn't really possible when working; who wanted to be accused of having been drinking before arguing about subs cases? Afterwards would be too late, so I thought better of it and got out my last frozen sausage and mash for dinner.

I got back to work for 9.30 p.m., took my long green Burton trench coat off and took a coffee into Anita's office.

'Hi there. You ok?'

'Why would I not be?' Her eyes flashed. She'd one of her blackish suits on and looked like a lawyer off an American TV programme.

'Just asking, no need to bite my head off.'

'Sorry, just getting to do subs night has required a lot of lobbying.'

'Not sure you'll think it's worthwhile when you've done some,' I joked. She looked sharply up at me standing in the doorway, ignoring my attempt at frivolity.

There was a knock on the door and the senior pay clerk came in, a big friendly guy called Tim who actually gave out the cash in the pay office for the subs we had signed for.

'Hiya both. Before you start, I've got five odd sick certificates to show you.' He leaned over and put them in front of Anita, and I moved round to the rear of the desk so I could also read them. She picked them up one at a time and then handed them to me to read.

I looked at them carefully,

'Well, all five are from the same surgery…'

'And what else?' Tim said.

'The stamps of the surgery address seem a bit amateur,' said Anita, so I looked again and nodded.

'My cousin happens to work at that surgery on the Scottie Road, so I rang her yesterday and she said they've lost a book of certificates, they weren't sure if they'd been stolen or just misplaced. There's no doctor with that name there either,' said Tim.

'So, someone's lifted the book of certificates and is giving or selling the certificates to their mates?' asked Anita.

'Who knows, that's your job not mine. I would say the stamp is a kid's one from Woolworths personally, but I'll leave you to it. I need to go and open the safe before the hordes arrive.'

Anita and I looked at each other, both thinking.

'We'll have no time to look at this tonight; I'll lock them in my desk, and we can meet first thing tomorrow?' I said. The queue was already lining up, so I went back to my office.

At a quarter to midnight, the queues had gone. I locked up my office and waited for Anita to finish with her final customer. Having been barked at earlier, I wanted to see if Anita would say how her evening had gone, but she didn't.

'Tomorrow can we discuss how we go about finding out who stole the sick note pad?' she said.

'Sure, I think I can manage that.' I looked at her out of the corner of my eye as we walked, she looked a bit tired for once and I forgave her the somewhat patronising question. We parted at the big car park, Anita still hadn't mentioned how the subs part of the evening had gone. The news on the way home was a piece on how British Leyland car workers' wives were encouraging their husbands to get back to work and end their massively long strike; it made me smile. That was a new angle so maybe things were finally changing for the better.

Arriving at work the next day I immediately noticed there was no noise or welding flashes from the factory floor. Instead of opening my office door, I went into the factory; nothing was moving at all. I went out and collared the first foreman I could see; there was clearly an issue in the Paint, Trim and Assembly (PTA) shop. It was always a relief when it wasn't an area where I was responsible for the industrial relations. I looked through Anita's door; she was wearing startling looking clothes. I knew literally nothing about clothes, but I knew they were not from M&S. I'd once seen a Jaeger label but was not sure how expensive they were anyway. I felt a little embarrassed as I had on my scruffy number two suit on with waistcoat, and felt I looked like a second-hand car salesman. A bit like second-hand car regulators, I couldn't break my student habits of cheap clothes. I indicated a coffee and she mouthed yes, so I took one in. As often happened, within a millisecond, she asked a business-focussed question.

'Do you think the sick note pad thief has given sick certificates away or is actually selling them?' I was slightly thrown.

'Umm, yes, well without interviewing them all, I can't see how we can honestly tell. Even then, I'm not sure they will grass each other up.'

'So, do you think it's gross misconduct like fraud or just a written warning like unauthorised absence?' said Anita over the top of her coffee. I sat down.

'Well, I'm not sure. Whoever stole the sick note pad, you could argue it's theft. Those using the notes are doing it fraudulently so you could argue the whole thing is a police matter.'

'Ok, we haven't seen it before, so let's go and see Bill and ask his advice,' said Anita and stood up to move.

'Hold on a minute, I'd rather we agreed what we think the options are, what the pros and cons are before we see Bill,' I said. I had noticed that Anita developed her views in conversations with others, and I was unsure if that was the way her mind worked, or it was some political thing to involve others. I had always wanted to be fully prepared as to my arguments before I started any difficult conversation, although I prided myself on actually listening and occasionally changing my mind.

'Let's put a "Do not disturb" up, pull the blinds down and spend fifteen minutes going through the options,' I said. Anita looked away, pained.

'Then we'll have to go through it again with Bill, that's not a great use of time.'

'Ok, five minutes then, a good personnel compromise,' I said. 'Look, if we want to follow the Ford blue book and be robot labour relations officers, let's call the police. But do we really want five people potentially sacked and criminalised, I don't. It's too harsh, in my view. I didn't join this company just to be a rule enforcer.'

'It might be right for one of them though,' said Anita, raising her eyebrows.

'I agree with you there. You know, look, I'd like to conduct an experiment, I've learnt to trust Lenny the steward whose area these are all in. I could say something like "Tell me who stole the pad and he's for the high jump but we'll treat the other four more lightly." If he can't deliver, we can say we'll have to involve the police.'

'But five jobs, surely he'll involve the convenor as no steward will come to a deal like that on their own,' argued Anita.

'Maybe, but that's a fair deal, it's generous to four of them. I looked in their records first thing, none of them have any form for anything.' Anita put down her coffee and looked at me.

'I think Liverpool is getting to you, you're going native. Ok, you go and see Bill then.'

'Let's go together' I said.

'It's your area, you do it,' and the conversation was clearly over. I shrugged and left, going to find my boss. Bill was sitting in his palatial office reading the day's press cuttings.

'Why is it when you appear you always look like a harbinger of doom? Fire away.' I went through the events of the previous night. Bill stroked his moustache as he listened intently to my proposal.

'What if the surgery involves the police, and the four you give out written warnings to are prosecuted?' said Bill. I had thought of this,

'The pay clerk's cousin works in the surgery, they don't know if they were lost or stolen.'

'Ok, so you are just trying to raise yourself up the popularity stakes with the stewards?' I wasn't sure if that was a serious comment or not but treated it seriously. 'Not at all. I just think five dismissals and five criminal records are four too many.' Bill nodded thoughtfully.

'You may have a point, but what if all five are selling them on and you set a new custom and precedent that we don't always dismiss for criminal prosecutions. Or what if the surgery involves the police for theft as that will also scupper your plan. Then you'll be for seeing the IRM for another development discussion. But it's on your head then if you want to do it that way. I think you'd better clear off before I change my mind. Let me know how it goes.'

'Cheers Bill,' I grimaced and left. Walking back to the piggeries, I was relieved, I was not sure I would have been prepared to go ahead with five dismissals if Bill had said no and I might have had to ask someone else to do the hearings in protest. I hated what was happening to the country right now, I hated the death wish that the unions seemed to have for the industry, but that didn't mean I would be happy kicking four men out just because I probably could. They had families like my own dad had. It wasn't what I'd signed up for and if I got it wrong sod it. Maybe I was in the wrong job after all.

I called in Lenny Lobo, showed him the five certificates, and laid out my proposal that Lenny give me the name of the guy who had stolen the certificate pad. If he didn't, the risk was police involvement and the hard-line company policy on criminal convictions and future employment for all five. Lenny was incredibly stressed by the conversation as soon as he saw the names on the certificates and left saying he would be back. I said time was of essence if they were to avoid the risk of five dismissals. I had just finished a separate case disciplinary letter when Willie John the convenor and Lenny appeared at the door, Lenny looking sheepish and Willie waved the sick certificates.

'We appreciate ye common sense approach to this wee perturbation.' He looked stern.

'Lenny here, he came to see me cos it's a bit complicated.'

'How's that then?' I said.

'Fred McManus admitted to thievin' the pad when the doctor turned his back and washed his hands.'

'Ok. And?'

'He's no longer with us. He resigned on the spot, Lenny here has his resignation letter, so ye can nae sack him as he's gone and left the plant already.'

'He can't, he needs to face a disciplinary…' I said.

'Too fuckin' late, laddie. He's already gone. Now here's the book of sick certificates he gave us.'

'Well, he's going down as an enforced termination then…'

'So, he'll no be getting a reference then, so what?' said Willie. 'The other four told Lenny that they took them for the Derby match night only, they could nae afford more time off with the strike and all.'

Lenny still looking sheepish said, 'If you suspend the others for three days and a final warning, I'll guarantee there's no appeal like.'

'Unless ye involve the rozzers,' said Willie, mischievously.

'I've told Lenny I won't be involving the police. My only worry is if the surgery does, then it's out of our hands,' I said.

'There'll no be a peep from our side, so the surgery will no find out the pad was stolen.' said Willie. 'Lenny will be the steward at the hearing.'

They stood up and moved towards the door, Willie turned round and said, 'You know, for someone that's a rabid young union basher, you're a strange skin you are. Aye, and that's a compliment.'

I sat open-mouthed, looking at the door closing behind them... Shit, that had not gone as planned, yet again. With my heart sinking I walked slowly towards Bill's office to let him know what had happened, that there would be no dismissal after all.

Bill started laughing, much to my chagrin as soon as I started relating the events.

'Willie probably told him to resign, he would have figured the surgery wouldn't know the medical sick certificates were here otherwise he wouldn't have offered the deal. Anyway, no harm done, the guy's left, you just lost a battery opportunity that's all.'

Although pleased Bill seemed to think the fact the guy had left was the main thing, I was pissed off as I would have liked to see him fired and felt outmanoeuvred by the union.

I was puzzled by the battery mention and asked Bill what he meant.

'When operators are dismissed for stealing car parts and batteries or whatever and get three months in jail, we put it on the notice boards to discourage the others.'

'Right,' I said and got up to go.

I found Lenny in my office hopping from one foot to another with nerves.

'Look, err, you've been fair with us and I wanted to be honest like, Willie made him resign to protect the others, there were four lads' jobs on the line.'

'I guessed that. I'm pissed off with it though. I need to think twice in future about trying to be helpful but I'm not blaming you. But be sure there's no loose talk; if it gets back to the surgery that he stole the book of certificates we're all in the khazi. By the way, the disciplinary for the other four is this afternoon,' I said. Lenny did a mock salute and left.

I needed to clear my head and went for a stroll round the factory. Along the first line I came to, a fork lift truck was moving a pallet of brackets to a subassembly area, where the under-body welders were hard at it in their chrome leather protective gear. I could smell the fumes and see the blue/yellow flashes. The individual jobs might be boring, but I was still fascinated by the process of putting a car together. I stopped for water in one of the tea rooms, sat down and looked around. No one was on relief, so it was empty. I shut my eyes for a moment, and opened them when I heard a banging on the glass, it was a gurning Jim O'Neill was looking in.

'Hard night was it, a skinful too far?' he said.

'I wish,' I said getting up and walked back with Jim relating his latest conspiracy theory about press shop management intrigue.

The disciplinary hearing went like clockwork until it came to the sanctions. The superintendent said in an adjournment that with sickness he could ill afford to lose four operators for three-day suspensions, so we reluctantly agreed on just the final warnings. After it was over, I went to see the pay clerk Ian, and let him know the outcome of the investigation. He accepted that it might be wise not to contact his relative who worked at the surgery or the company might be severely embarrassed if the police were called. Ian was relieved there would be no involvement for him and pleased some form of justice had been meted out. It was just me that was unsatisfied with the outcome. I consoled myself that although I had been worked over again by the union, I'd saved four lads' jobs. But it was almost like I kept getting penalised for trying to do the right thing by people. At the end of the day, I didn't want to ruin four families' lives and I'd at least got that result.

Flag burner

I knew there was going to be a vote of confidence in parliament but also knew that no government had lost one since Ramsay MacDonald in 1923 or 1924. I'd not given it that much thought. I knew the Lib–Lab pact had failed last year, but I'd not kept up with the news that the Scottish National Party had put down a motion of no confidence and the Tories had taken this over. How a nationalist party was voting with one opposed to devolution puzzled me. The fact remained that the Labour government had lost by one vote and there would be a general election. I hoped, given the appalling winter the country had suffered and the moronic ways the trade unions had chosen to act, that the Labour Party would be punished at the polls. To even hear myself think this was no longer a shock; I'd spent the last year passionately hectoring shop stewards about how their stupid short-termist behaviour would damage investment and their future.

I wanted to see my college friend Pete, who worked for a left wing think tank, to discuss the ramifications of an election. I had argued about politics with Pete every day at college, and an election was just the excuse I needed for a night out. With the exception of the *Mirror* and the *Guardian*, most of the press was now anti-trade union, and the country was surely moving rightwards. We arranged to meet that evening in Yates Wine Lodge, but when we got there it was rammed with two raucous hen parties, so we walked on to the Philharmonic in Hardman Street.

As soon as I opened the ornate Victorian door, I saw Anita with my boss Bill sitting together in the corner. I stopped, frozen, and Pete stumbled into the back of me. The moment of panic passed, I waved, Bill waved back, and Anita smiled wanly. I walked away from them over to the bar, slowly.

'Are you alright?' said Pete.

'Yes, just someone I knew, or thought I knew.' I sat down as Pete went to the bar, choosing the chair with my back to Bill and Anita. My mind was in overdrive with all sorts of shit; should I introduce Pete to them, should I have asked to join them? Pete sat down. 'Frank, I told you the "Social Contract" wouldn't work in the end, didn't I?'

'What…?' I said.

'What's up with you?'

'Oh, sorry Pete…'

Bill interrupted us, on his way to the toilet.

'All right Frank, who's this then?'

'Oh Bill, Pete, we were at college together; he's a researcher for a left wing think tank.'

'Another leftie then?' he mocked.

Before I could engage my brain, I said, 'I didn't know you were seeing Anita.'

'I'm happily married.' Giving me a withering look, Bill walked away.

'Oh' was all I could whisper. I looked away embarrassed, I could see, in the reflection of a polished brass mirror, Anita writing notes. Pete looked at me, looked at Anita and said, 'Am I missing something here?'

I had a pull of my beer but didn't reply so Pete shrugged and said, 'Listen, you know I'm doing a paper on the party politics of shop stewards so tell me how political your lot are?'

I tried to focus.

'Mostly not at all, it's local pay and terms and conditions they are interested in 90% of the time. I'm mentoring a couple of stewards on a WEA course, but it's like Sociology 101. The real union leaders in the factory just read the *Sun* backwards and the *Racing Post*.'

'Surely there must be active Labour Party members, you know, stewards who want to be MPs and the like?' asked Pete.

'Honestly, I've not met one. They hardly bother to go to union branch meetings and our never-ending aggravation has done nothing to politicise them that I can see.' Bill and Anita interrupted us.

'We're off now see you on Monday,' said Bill. I started to stand up,

'Oh Anita, this is Pete, a friend from college.'

Anita looked at me, stony faced with pursed lips.

'Hi, yes, Bill told me. Nice to meet you,' and left without looking again.

'She's a bit harsh,' said Pete. I said nothing. It didn't take a genius to realise Bill had probably mentioned my earlier comment. I wished I could just disappear down the nearest hole. 'Gordon Bennett,' I muttered to myself, the rest of the evening remained a blur.

I'd had very few real girlfriends and they were not slow in implying I wasn't emotionally sensitive. I knew in my heart that was probably the case, but I mostly blamed it on my parents who, like many of their generation, had lived through the events of the last war. I shuddered as I remembered my mum telling me about the cattle train full of bodies stopping by mistake in Luton station while she was there, victims from the Coventry air raid. I remembered my Dad crying at the *Cruel Sea* film on television when a Destroyer depth-charged their own sailors because there was thought to be a German U-boat beneath them in the sea.

'We did that once,' my Dad had said in a sombre voice. It just meant my parents had become stoic, hardened even, though they had not talked much about the war. To be alive with a job, a warm house and a family was enough out of life for them. I desperately wanted to be a warmer person, not just for work and relationships but also because I'd begun to feel I was missing out on being a fully rounded person. Anyway, I knew I would not have the nerve to say any of that to Anita and cringed in the car at the thought of it. I was sometimes jealous of the public-school twats I'd met, with their carefully honed social skills even though many of them were as thick as the office wall. With no sisters, and a mother who was loving but as hard as nails, my teenage years were spent in the local library trying to educate myself, playing sports or fighting. I knew I couldn't hide behind my upbringing forever, if I really wanted to change, I would have to get on and do it myself.

There was a long queue on the Speke Road for some reason, so I dawdled along, unable to shake my melancholic mood. I knew I was different from many of my school friends. I remembered a girl from a neighbouring school talking to me about a *Coronation Street* plot on TV and being clueless. She didn't believe me and had called over a friend to see if I really didn't know or was just taking the mick. I had never forgotten the look of disbelief on the girl's face, like I was from another planet.

I finally reached work after a long delay. On the way to opening the office door I stopped for a second to listen for the noise of the factory working, it was reassuringly there. I slumped back in my chair and opened my desk diary to remind myself what I had on that day. There was a tapping on the window, and I looked up to see Anita asking in sign language did I want a coffee? I jumped up and did thumbs up sign and smiled.

She walked in with two coffees and I noticed she looked stunning in a dark green trouser suit.

'How was your weekend?' and she sat down and handed me the yucky coffee. I was naturally a bit defensive, because of my faux pas with Bill.

'Had a great time dissecting the upcoming election with Pete but that was about it unless you count faggots and chips. It was strange seeing you in the pub though.' She looked directly into my face. 'Yes, Bill said you thought we were an item.' I could feel myself redden.

'I, I, just asked that's all.' Anita stayed staring, relishing how uncomfortable I was becoming. She finally laughed, relieving the tension.

'I was just getting some career advice on transferring to Head Office or resigning.'

'Are you?'

'Am I what?'

'Leaving.'

'No. He persuaded me not to, at least for the time being.'

I breathed out slowly. 'Well, I'm glad to hear that. It wouldn't be the same if you go.'

'I've been here a lot longer than you, and I don't want to stay a minute longer than I need to.'

I frowned, 'I keep forgetting how ambitious you are.'

'For a woman?'

'And that. I guess people I know just work, rather than it always being a step on to a bigger job.'

Anita changed the topic. 'Bill told me about your Friday night excitement.'

She really was so nosy.

'It was properly funny, a cross between Benny Hill and a military operation.'

'He said you requested me there rather than Tim, I'm not sure whether I should feel flattered?' she innocently enquired.

'Well, I just thought Tim was too new, but actually he did fine. I guess Bill was concerned what would happen at a porn show in the factory if it kicked off and there was a fracas.'

'It didn't sound like I missed anything that exciting, but what a place this is,' she said.

Before I could think it through and lose courage I said, 'Listen, would you be up for another day out sometime? I really enjoyed that film day we had.'

'Maybe.'

There was a loud knock on the door and Johnnie Murphy the Welfare PO burst in, so Anita stood up to leave. I had time to look her in the face again before dealing with a distressed Johnnie.

'Maybe,' she repeated with a playful smile.

Johnnie looked at Anita then me before blurting out, 'Message from Eric, come quick, one of your lads is burning a flag outside…'

'Flag?' I said. I knew there were some Japanese car parts suppliers visiting that day, but I was not involved. I could smell the burning as soon as I got outside the office into the front reception car park. I could see a security guard extinguishing a burning Japanese flag near the bottom of a flagpole. A number of senior managers were standing at the foot of another flagpole which was flying the Union Jack. They were lining up as a VIP car was approaching from the gates and they looked agitated.

'Get that fuckin' flag removed and put the company flag in its place,' the plant manager shouted furiously. Bill Budd and a security officer had an older guy in a strong grip, it was a lead discer I vaguely recognised. He was crying gently. Harry Wolfson pointed at me and shouted, 'Get him to your fuckin' office, lock the door and read him the riot act – be quick about it.'

I was shocked to hear the plant manager swear and grabbed the man from Bill. He was in his late fifties, small and emaciated looking. I guided him quickly towards my office, followed by the security officer. I could see dozens of office staff staring out of the windows fronting the car park.

Bill jogged alongside. 'He set fire to the Japanese flag, and then started crying. We've just avoided a diplomatic incident by stopping the visitors at the barrier. Harry wants him fired right now,' and rolled his eyes upwards.

I guided the flag-burner into the building as two big black limousines came through the gates. I sat him down in my office and let him be for a moment; he took a deep breath and sighed. The door opened and Johnnie, the Welfare P.O. came in with three teas, which I found undrinkable but Sam, the lead discer, sipped at. He was ashen-faced.

'Just start at the beginning when you can,' I said softly.

'The bastards. I... I... was captured in Singapore and they tortured us for years. I was on my way to the medical centre for a routine lead measurement and I saw it... the flag. Cruel bastard Nips. They beat my best mate to death in Burma with bamboo poles, I owe it to him, sack me if you have to.'

'Ok. Ok. We understand. But that was over thirty years ago, you must be seeing Datsun cars and Sony stereos and other Japanese stuff everyday...'

'It's just the flag, I can't stand it, it brings it all back and makes me sick to the stomach.'

He was slumped over with his body shaking like he was in shock. Johnnie sat next to him and put his arm around him.

'What exactly did you do?' I said, as sympathetically as I could. He looked tearfully up from his tea and said,

'The security man had laid it out to attach it, I rushed over grabbed it ran off and set fire to it with my lighter.'

'Bloody hell Sam, you could be in mega trouble here. Listen, who is your steward so I can get him along?'

'They beat him to death with bamboo poles...'

I cut across, 'Look, would you prefer to see the nurse, or Johnnie here can run you home?' He indicated the latter.

'Ok then, now could you be in for ten o'clock tomorrow as there will have to be an enquiry of sorts, but I'll do my best to ensure management understand the background.'

Johnnie took over consoling Sam who was still breathing faintly. I went to personnel records to check his file – nothing, not even a bloody warning for lateness. I could see the way it would pan out in the morning. I thought through the harsh disciplinary possibilities; it would potentially be something like wilful destruction of company property/ conduct prejudicing the future of the business/endangering the factory by fire... the list could be endless if management wanted it so.

'Bugger, bugger,' I whispered to myself at a desk in the records department. I sat back and looked at the ceiling, I knew without even thinking it through that I would go out on a limb for him. He'd been tortured for God's sake. I knew the odds were stacked against Sam given the gravity of the incident, and what the plant manager had publicly said. I looked again at his file and had the beginnings of an idea. If I could get him signed off psychiatrically unfit, I might be able to get a medical discharge with no loss of pension. That thought cheered me up, so I got up to visit the occupational physician to see if the idea might have legs. I knew that the plant manager wanted him sacked and crossing him could be a personal disaster for me. There was a sharp knock and Lenny and Willie John burst in to the records office.

Willie spoke, 'Heard you were up here. The whole factory has heard about it, bloody idiot, but what's the score? The man is harmless I tell ye.'

I looked over.

'He was tortured by the Japs, after Singapore. I'm thinking he must be mentally scarred so I'm trying to hatch a plot to save him. I had better say no more, I might not succeed. If I do, he'll see the medic and we can suspend the disciplinary tomorrow.'

Willie looked at me and nodded sagely, 'Aye, that sounds a fair one to me.' Lenny looked worried but said nothing and they both departed as quickly as they had arrived.

I walked over to the medical centre, thinking as I went. The lad's card was marked, as they say in Liverpool, the plant manager would not directly interfere, but the dismissing manager would know his view. I desperately tried to remember a recent article in the paper about soldiers from Belfast in the Northern Irish troubles, who had something beginning to be called post-traumatic stress disorder. Like delayed shellshock, surely this could be such a case, just with a thirty-year delay.

Dr Abbott the medic was oldish and an expert in occupational hygiene topics like lead poisoning, solvent issues and the like. I had no idea if he knew anything about shellshock.

'Doc, thanks for seeing me. Look, I know normally when we meet, I'm trying to work up a solid case so some lag is dismissed after months of skiving off sick with previous multiple warnings.'

'That sounds about right,' he said in his clipped BBC English. 'As you know, my first duty is to my patients.'

'Well, I want to save someone from being fired for once,' I said. The Doc raised his shaggy Denis Healey eyebrows and listened intently as I explained what had happened at the flagpole.

'Well, that is a first. Now, we have an excellent consultant psychiatrist we pay a retainer to so I'll talk to him. I know he recently gave a talk on the post-war stress suffered by American GIs in Vietnam, he's an expert in this field.'

'Well, if I can suspend tomorrow's hearing because you send him home psychiatrically unwell, there must be a chance of an ill health retirement rather than the sack for gross misconduct?'

The doctor nodded and agreed, so we shook hands and I thought about next steps on the way back to the office. The flag ceremony would shortly be over, and I definitely did not want to meet Bill or any senior production person. They would surely not agree with the plan and the man would be sunk without trace. Better not to ask and just spring it on them tomorrow, I thought. Absolutely no one would cross the plant manager lightly and to be fair, it was a serious incident. But the guy had been tortured, he was acting way out of character and deserved another chance in my eyes.

I deliberately kept out of the way and left early, noticing two notes from Bill's secretary on my desk summoning me to meetings. I left them there, like I'd not read them.

When I got home, I agonised about what to do and finally rang Anita.

'Hi. Are you alone?'

'Yes, a bit conspiratorial for you?'

'Listen, will you go along and tell Bill I've had a domestic crisis and had to leave early but will be in first thing tomorrow. Secondly, will you meet me after to work to discuss something career threatening I'm going to do about the flag burner?'

'Why can't you talk to Bill?'

'I can't explain now, but I can't talk to Bill.'

'Oh, so I'm second choice then?'

'No, you are my valued bloody colleague and he is my boss. How about six, usual pub?'

'Ok.'

Anita walked into the Childe of Hale looking as fresh as a daisy. I bought her a sparkling water and moved to a quiet area of the pub. I went through the incident in all the detail, though much of it seemed pretty public due to the combination of Johnnie Murphy and the sheer number of people who had seen a lot by just looking out of the office windows.

Anita frowned, and put on her business school/big sister face.

'It's not very professional. You're trying to engineer an outcome based on one side of the story; you know we don't do that in personnel. What's the management view...?'

'The plant manager's was shouted out for all to hear...'

'No, considered management view. Bill will go mad, he'll think you've not only exceeded your authority but will see through you avoiding a hearing anyway,' she added.

'But if the lad leaves with an unreduced pension, surely that's a win–win isn't it?'

'I'm not sure it is,' as she sipped her water looking over the rim of the glass at me.

I took a mouthful of beer.

'I'll resign if I have to. I'm not letting a tortured war veteran be sacked with no pension, no references over this. With all the shysters we have employed here right now. No way. Completely unjust.'

'Well, I can see you feel strongly but I don't think it's very professional circumventing our personnel policy, and you're being disloyal to Bill who recruited you.'

We chatted about other things for a while, then Anita said she'd got to go to wash her hair. That phrase had always puzzled me, but I understood the message.

To cap it all, the car wouldn't start and I had to get a taxi home, so I took the battery with me to charge that evening. I was well pissed off by the time I got in, notwithstanding the expense of the taxi.

That evening I cooked a frozen Cornish pasty and chips. It was inedible. I sat at my Formica table and looked out over the grim car park. I knew I had the best of intentions, he was my dad's war fighting generation. If I failed the guy, at least I would have tried to do what was right. I played myself to sleep with 'Another Brick in the Wall' by Pink Floyd on the portable cassette player. It summed up my pessimistic mood that night. Or was it another nail in my coffin?

The next morning, after collecting the car by taxi, I was in early. Bill was there waiting for me, smoking and looking angry.

'Look, it's not acceptable to leave a message that you're going home like that, you have to speak to me, have you got that?

'Oh sorry, yes...'

'Right, make sure you do in future. Anyway, put that to one side. The public affairs manager has been down, Granada Reports TV and the *Liverpool Echo* are asking him if a war veteran is being sacked today. Eric wants it fixing so the flag-burner causes no publicity.'

I looked at Bill, trying to stop a smile appearing in the corner of my mouth *(I was saved!)*

'Is the plant manager ok with that? Half the site heard what he said to me by the flagpole,' I said.

'Do you think he wants this kind of publicity? I can see the headline now... something

like 'Company sacks war veteran after Japanese flag brings back war horrors.'

'You missed your vocation Bill, there'll be a job for you on the *Sun*,' I laughed, relieved.

'Oi, don't be cheeky. Can you fix it then, Mr lateral thinker?'

'As it happens, I have a plan that may make the problem go away to our mutual satisfaction...'

'What?' Bill said, suspiciously.

'Dr Abbott is seeing the flagman at nine o'clock. If he diagnoses a mental breakdown, that may be enough for a medical retirement, given his age.'

'Umm, that sounds good to me. If you can square that off with the stewards, I'll tell production management that is what we are trying for and to keep their noses out on this one. Hold on a minute, you mean you've arranged this before I told you about the PR view just now?'

'Yeah,' I said, innocently. Bill glared at me and left the office. I jumped in the air with a 'Yahoo…' the gods were on my side for once. I went to find the stewards before Sam came in to see the doctor; they were in Willie John's press shop convenor's office. Much bigger than my own I noted.

'Right, the good news is that Sam is seeing the Doc right now and hopefully he'll be signed off indefinitely so we can move to a medical health retirement.'

'Yeah, great… listen, we appreciate what you are trying to do here, but the nigger in the woodpile, no offence Lenny, is he wants to stay.'

'None taken,' said Lenny.

'His wife has died, he's no bairns, and has nothing else to do,' said Willie.

'Christ guys, it's not his decision. If the medic says he is unfit for work, he's unfit for work. Most of your lads would give their right arm for an immediate pension with no actuarial reduction.'

'We know, we know, we'll make sure he leaves ok but it's not goin' to be easy,' said Lenny.

'By the way, have you been in contact with the PR manager?' I asked.

'Who's he when he's at home?' said Willie. I eyeballed him and was quite sure he hadn't. So how exactly did the media get the story? I had one other idea.

Dr Abbot was as good as his word, and immediately referred Sam to the psychiatrist for future evaluation, so I was able to call off the disciplinary hearing. The situation was not yet resolved but the immediate crisis was over. I went to brief Bill.

'That's a job well done that is. Eric is impressed. I didn't mention you had decided on it without knowing about the PR threats,' and looked questioningly at me. I was pleased to have got a good result for the guy but kicked myself that I'd let it slip it was planned before hearing the PR news. It hadn't worked out the way I'd expected but I was happy, especially after the difference of opinion with Anita. What was it Napoleon had said about lucky generals? I breathed a long sigh of relief.

That evening I'd agreed to meet Pete in Aigburth, as a date for an election in May had now been called. With the exception of NUPE and NALGO strikes in public services, most of the strikes were now over. Even the civil servants, who had been doing disruptive one day strikes since February, had settled – for an astronomical deal mind you – 26% over two years. Although I was initially in a good mood because of the day's events, the evening did not go well. Pete took exception, after two pints, to my support for the Conservative party leader Thatcher's proposals on closed shops and secondary action. Pete's final, 'Frank, you're a Tory wanker,' shouted out in frustration brought the bar to a near silence.

I immediately responded.

'And just why are Labour losing all the by-elections? I'll tell you why, because normal people are sick of all this union rhetoric, they can see a bunch of selfish bastards a mile off.'

Peter got up, grabbed his coat and stormed out. I shouted at him as he left, 'They don't want your new Jerusalem, they want a new Cortina!' and he was embarrassed when two or three people gave me a clap.

I stayed to finish my pint; we had fallen out before and it would not be a problem. I took the *Telegraph* from the paper rack beside the table and started to read it. I nearly went looking for Pete when I read the editorial: '1950 German manufacturing world share of exports 7%, Britain 25%. 1974 German share 22%, Britain 7%.' I put it back in the rack in disgust. I had also just told Pete I would not be going to the 'Rock against Racism' concert, worthy cause though it was. That had brassed Pete off even more.

I picked up dinner at a supermarket and drove home. I was worried I was near the alcohol limit so drove very carefully. I was maudlin that evening and had to stop myself from ringing Anita. I didn't because she was too disconcerting, she seemed to understand my feelings before I even did myself. I also knew that whenever I had a few pints I could be a pain in the arse, and I didn't want to be apologising for that at some later date.

I looked around the flat, the bookshelves on bricks with no proper bed and no sofa. I needed to do something about it if I was ever to invite Anita back, but I was still a graduate trainee and not paid much at all. I didn't even have a Hoover, just a dustpan and brush. Anyway, I knew the flag burning result that day was fortuitous and it could have gone very differently for me indeed.

I was still not sure if the job was for me, so not putting down too many costly roots was surely wise, but maybe I should invest in a proper bed after I had bought a newer car anyway. My concern last night that I might have to resign over the flag-burner, had led to me subconsciously considering other options. I'd once thought of being a social worker like many of the 'Hooray Henrys' on the university course. The trouble was, I had lived most of my life amongst the urban working class, so I knew how some of them behaved after a few pints down their local. I'd seen it in my own extended family. I also liked the idea of teaching. I had benefitted from two or three inspirational teachers at my own crap school. But I couldn't see myself teaching in a class where very few had any real interest in learning anything; I knew I would eventually lose my temper and thump someone. I understood the sociology of it, but that wouldn't make it any easier to do. The thought of teaching in a public school had once attracted me, other than I had never been in one in my life to date. My knowledge was based solely on reading Mathew Arnold, George Orwell and Evelyn Waugh. I had met some seriously clever people from public schools but most of them just had better social skills. I knew my own schooling had certain limitations, but it had at least left me resilient, unbullyable and handy with my fists.

I had begun to realise recently that there was one other difference, possibly because of my background. I had been surprised by the deference to authority that existed in the world of work, whereas I had always defied authority when I thought it right. Although I was not that proud of my teenage behaviour, the fact that no one had ever expected anything from me had made me a free agent. No family expectations determined my behaviour; it was always my personal choice. If I could have changed anything, I would have gone to more school discos, northern soul parties and spent a bit less time in the library. It might have improved my relationships with girls. I realised I was no further forward with my career dilemma, but it was at least not an immediate problem. Monday would at least bring something new; labour relations were refreshingly unpredictable.

On Monday morning I was greeted by the usual smell of welding fumes and white spirit. I bumped into Jim at the Klix machine, smirking conspiratorially.

'Bill and Eric reckon you did good with the mad flag-burner. Me, I smell something fishy about the way you handled it,' and touched his nose. As I had been tied up with the flag-burner case, Jim had had to handle the porn show disciplinaries so updated me. The foreman had been summarily dismissed by staff personnel (as he was a white-collar employee) and seven operators were given first written warnings, as they all claimed they had permission to be in the plant room. One more should have been dismissed under totting up procedure because of previous warnings still in time, but it was reduced to a final warning and three-day suspension on appeal. I shrugged and went back into my office. Before I could weigh up Jim's barbed comment, Anita appeared in her long camel hair coat.

'Hi, Frank what you are doing for the next fifteen?'

'Nothing why?' She brought her coffee into my office, with her coat still on, shut the door and sat down.

'So…'

'So what?' I replied.

'How did you get senior management to change their minds on the flag-burner?' I was slightly disappointed, hoping for something more personal, but concealed it.

'I didn't. PR did. They said TV and radio were going to run a story on us sacking a hero POW.' She looked at me intensely, her black eyes boring into me.

'You know Anita, you're as bad as Jim, always looking for some dodgy angle.'

'And why should I think that?' she smiled slowly, undoing her coat at the same time.

'Look, I know you think I have a partial regard to management instructions, but I am not sly like Jim you know.'

Bill Budd marched in without knocking, looking curiously from Anita to me.

'Sorry to break up your morning tete-a-tete, but there's a planning meeting on the body sides productivity initiative that you should have been invited to, it's in five minutes in the conference room upstairs.' He looked at us again quizzically and backed out of the door, leaving it open.

We sat there, both holding our brown plastic Klix cups. I frowned and said, 'Did you see that look he gave us?'

'Yeah, I think he thinks we are seeing each other,' her eyes twinkling in the gloom.

'Are we?'

'Maybe.'

'Would you like to go for a drive on Sunday?'

'In your car?!' she laughed.

'You had better go, umm, I'll pick you up in my car, noon Sunday then,' she said.

'Really?' I said, taken aback.

'But lunch is on you.'

'Deal.'

'You had better be off to your meeting then.'

— **13** —

Bullock

One gloomy Friday, there was a knock on my office door.

'Mr Pramlad, I'm Jack press shop A shift steward, wondered if I could 'ave a word?'

'Go ahead,' I said.

'The convenor said you might be able to help me wif somat, like. I'm on a course and 'ave to write the Bullock Report up.'

'So, I'm the T and G Union education officer am I now?' Jack squirmed on his seat.

'Willie says there's a pamphlet that the Dagenham stewards wrote about it, but he can't find it right now. He thinks it said we should nationalise industries like cars and trucks and there was no question of sitting on boards and the like. He said you seemed to know about it from an argument you had with him.'

I was delighted at the diversion from my depressing meetings and realised for the first time the stewards saw me as some strange academic. I warmed to the argument,

'Right, so, you nationalise them without compensation like the *Morning Star* says. Where's the money for the new model coming from?'

'Err, the government I suppose.'

'This is on top of the money they're finding for British Leyland, Rolls Royce, NVT and so on. That will be two pence on the pound in your tax,' I said.

'I did say to Willie that the Germans sit on works councils and the like, and they're being paid more than us with better holidays as well.'

I began to think that if this job was not really going to work out, maybe I should be an academic for the WEA. Maybe the pros and cons of the Bullock Report suited me more than the daily grind of people issues in personnel work; I had recently thought that personnel would be alright if it wasn't for the people!

'Our WEA lecturer is saying there may be some European law soon that makes it compulsory for workers to be on boards like in West Germany.'

'Yeah, maybe in twenty years' time. Remember they don't actually have closed shops in Germany, you can be on a supervisory board and not be a union member.'

'Well management agreed to union closed shops here like,' said the steward.

'I know that but if you asked them would they like a return to the cosy beer and sandwiches with full time union officials like they had in the sixties or local shop steward committees like now, which do you think they would go for?'

'Yeah, well. Ta, that's 'elpful that is. How come youse the only one that's heard of it?'

'I'm not. I'm pretty certain some of the senior management people here gave evidence to the committee writing it. Remember that there was a minority report and the radicals in the Institute for Workers' Control rejected it. It's few years ago now, but I have some college notes I can look at as well. I think you had to be a union member to have a vote on who the board worker reps would be, which caused an issue. Anyway, have a go at an answer then bring it in to see me one lunchtime, I'll look it over for you.'

'Cheers, I'll buy you a pint sometime.'

'Careful Jack, you don't want to be seen socialising with management, you'll not get re- elected.' We both laughed together, and Jack departed.

At 4 p.m., a time when staff could decently leave, especially after a particularly shitty week, Bill Budd slid his head round the door.

'All the POs are meeting at the Childe for a quick birthday drink for Johnnie.' I looked up and before I could ask if Anita would be there, Bill read my mind,

'Even Anita's coming,' and backed out of the door still smiling. I looked for Anita, but she was out on the factory floor, now routine in our jobs. I hadn't been able to make arrangements for our Sunday date yet, and I certainly did not want her to see inside my flat.

Anita waved as I entered the pub, she'd put lipstick on which she never wore at work. Next to her was Johnnie going on about dog racing and Tim listening politely in his animated vacant, posh boy way. I would rescue her soon, after I got a much-needed drink.

Jim collared me at the bar,

'I hear you're up shit creek on the drilling manning,' he smirked. I knew in my heart he was probably right but was in no mood for Jim's carping criticism after a week of dispute meetings.

'Well, I've an idea for a paddle,' I said winking at the same time. Jim fingered his greasy hair parting,

'What, what? You're planning something, I know you I trained you,' said Jim.

'You mean you tried to.'

Jim looked faintly hurt, he was a fixer with few principles at all and would offer anything to get short-term results. I respected Jim's skills for certain situations, but it had led to short-termism; the current manning issue was partly due to Jim's previous model run out fix.

Bill put down his drinks tray and announced , 'Just thought I would let you know that between us, we've lost 247 cars this week, an unofficial record when there's not been one formal strike. Anyway, let's not talk about work as we've all had enough this week, let's talk about the big match instead. Widnes will thrash St Helens tomorrow!'

Everyone laughed; no one followed rugby league except 'woollybacks,' people born in places like Widnes and Warrington at least five miles away. He'd changed the mood for the better and I could hear Johnnie telling Anita how feeding a racing dog a pork pie before a race would nobble the dog and get the odds up for the next one. Bill proposed a toast to Johnnie and then Jim had to leave to take his kids to Scouts, so we moved onto one table and I could sit next to Anita.

'How are you? I've not seen you this week,' I said.

'I've been offsite half of the week at a supervisor's assessment centre at the Adelphi.'

'Sounds better than my week, that's for sure. Any good candidates?'

'You know, usual white men whose main qualification is being good at their current line job. Hardly any have an education, hardly any have leadership skills so I'm unimpressed.' I was intrigued with this radical view and said, 'So, you think the calibre of the foremen is a big part of our strikes problem?'

'I would like to experiment with the odd graduate, MBA, some mixed race and even foreigners. A bit of diversity might shake things up.'

Bill was listening in and laughed, 'When you can earn triple in a consultancy, why would any MBA do a foreman's job here?'

'It's a good leadership experience if it's done well. Same for women, but unless women are actually employed on the shop floor, I can't see there will ever be women foremen.'

'But most women don't want to work shifts, what with childcare responsibilities. I've not seen a single application in my time, for any of the production jobs,' I said.

'There aren't even any women's toilets on the factory floor Frank,' said Anita.

'Are there not? I didn't know that. Maybe we should positively encourage more women, the jobs aren't physically that hard anymore just bloody boring, though the unions won't like it.'

'Well, today's *Mail* says half the country sees the existence of unions as a bad thing, though you can't always believe what you read in the papers,' said Anita.

'They're out of control,' added Bill. 'You'd think Ron Todd would be a stronger leader after twenty years at Ford Dagenham, wouldn't you? He's doing nothing at the T and G.'

'I missed all the miners' strike stuff in the early seventies that brought Heath to his knees,' continued Anita. 'It's a bit better now than the dead of last winter, but I haven't seen any real improvement in this country since the end of the big union strikes,' the longest political statement I had heard Anita make.

'I wonder if all the union pickets are going to get their comeuppance in the election, seems fifty–fifty looking at the polls. Maybe if it wasn't for Thatcher being so shrill, they might be further ahead,' I said. Tim then came in, 'How about you Bill, you've been around the longest, who do you think will win?'

Bill responded, 'I read the *Times* review of the Tory manifesto yesterday, and there is no mention of banning secondary picketing or outlawing the closed shop. So, there's not much that would have helped us here since the November strikes. The no strike contracts for firemen and gravediggers will go down well though.'

Johnnie looked up from rolling a fag,

'This new lot, the Moss Evans and Ron Todds, they didn't fight in the Spanish Civil War like Jack Jones, and he was a proper community socialist on our docks like. I've no time for them, they think of no one but themselves, but I'd choke before I would vote Tory. '

I nodded and said, 'Isn't he the guy some joker said about the Labour Party "Vote Jack Jones, cut out the middleman".' Everyone laughed.

Eventually the discussion petered out, Bill, Tim and Johnnie departed leaving Anita and me together. Before I could talk one to one with Anita, she looked at her watch and said, 'I'm meeting the girl I used to room with at eight o'clock, so I'll have to go. I'll see you at noon Sunday then. Be ready.' She got up, touched my arm gently and left.

I drove the few miles home stopping off at the Chinese at the bottom of the road for sweet and sour pork. I'd bought a TV aerial cable one lunchtime to try and get the small black and white to work properly but fell asleep from tiredness before I could even fit it.

I visited my local greasy spoon for a fried breakfast first thing Saturday, after buying the three main political party manifestos in WH Smiths. Over my tea, I compared the words and promises with my harsh personal experiences of the last twelve months. Despite my personal misgivings about Thatcher, I thought the Tories had the right approach to the unions which was the existential issue facing the country right now. The recent anarchy caused by the public service unions should never be repeated. I thought the Liberals, who had been different in the early seventies looked like a spent force. As for Labour, the manifesto was more of the same failed policies. I momentously decided, after eating the fried bread, that I would actually vote Tory the Thursday of the election. I leaned back and thought of the consequences, what it implied about my life now and what the car industry had done for my politics. My college friends would be choking on their Newcastle Brown.

Sunday finally arrived, and right on time Anita. I was worried about how smart Anita would be when she arrived, she'd a new looking red skirt and an orangey Laura Ashley top on. I greeted her warmly at the flat door and was putting my old but still reasonable Crombie overcoat on at the door, when she pointed at my hall corridor wall.

'I didn't realise you liked embroidery.'

I looked round embarrassed, and anxious to close the front door.

'I don't. That's half a National Front banner I ripped up at a student demo a few years ago.'

'Really? So, you are proud enough of it to frame it?'

'Well, yes I suppose so it's only a cheap frame.' I could feel myself reddening a little.

'Yet you're not voting Labour on Thursday?'

'I don't see a contradiction, do you? You know at the pub last night, I finally decided that I'm a social Liberal and economic Tory,' more defensively than I wanted it to sound. I added, 'That's what working for this company has done for me.'

We walked down the steps to where her car was parked, the only new one in the car park.

'Do you fancy lunch in Chester on the river?' I asked as we got in the car.

'Isn't it a bit cold?'

'Well, in a pub not actually on the river as such,' I replied.

Anita smiled as we drove out and turned left.

'Gateacre would be quite nice if it wasn't for the rubbishy infill houses,' she said, as we drove out.

'Like where I live?'

'Definitely.'

We both looked left at the giant Ford car plant, our eyes drawn to it, the steam from the boiler house and the huge mushroom fire tower dominating the view. Anita's new car purred along quietly and when we reached the outskirts of Chester, I directed her past the convent and down to the river. We walked along to the Boathouse Inn and I did a John Cleese walk as an excuse to link arms.

We managed to get a seat overlooking the river, as a rowing eight went slowly by. I tried to rub the condensation off the windows and went to the bar for drinks.

'It's really nice to be out with you again,' I said. She squeezed my hand and smiled without saying anything. I looked at her perfect light brown complexion and teeth and had to restrain myself from just leaning over and kissing her. The fish and chips came and were not bad for an English pub, at least not in a basket.

I asked her between mouthfuls, how she would be voting in the election on Thursday.

'As my dad tells me to.'

I choked on my fish and, coughing, searched her face for the joke, but couldn't see any.

'Well, my mum will certainly vote as he advises.'

'That must be illegal,' I muttered.

'Yeah Frank, you don't know how lucky you are,' said Anita seriously.

'You could have fooled me,' I replied.

'But you are an entirely free person, your family has no expectations of you, and you live only for yourself.'

'God, you make me sound so selfish.'

'Well, I'm not an entirely free party like you.'

I looked at her puzzled, but sensing her seriousness decided not to reply.

'So how are you voting then?' I asked.

'I'm not saying, that's my right isn't it?' she laughed, crossing her arms. I glanced at her and as her moods fluctuated quickly, I was damned if I knew what the trigger was for her sudden frostiness. I suggested we walk to the cathedral, as she'd never been inside. I agonised over whether to link arms again on the way but decided against it. I didn't want to risk spoiling the rest of the day by being rejected. We wandered around the sandstone Norman cathedral and I pointed out the old Army colours hanging from the walls, one dating from the Cheshire Regiment fighting in the American War of Independence.

'You like history, don't you?' remarked Anita, warmly.

'Yeah, I guess I always have,' I said as I gazed around the wonderful building.

We walked around the city walls for a while, chatting away till it got cold and then we walked back to the car and started the drive back. As we drove over the Runcorn bridge towards Liverpool Anita said, 'Shall we stop for a proper filter coffee at the Childe?'

'Yeah, great idea, it's Romboud's there. We'll have about half an hour before they close.'

We pulled into the car park. The Sunday lunch families were just leaving and apart from the odd serious drinker, we were alone. I really liked the pub, it was a kind of oasis in the countryside but very near work, no more than a ten-minute drive. It had probably not changed much in 150 years looking at the photos on the wall, the panelling and ceilings looked exactly the same. Anita insisted on buying the coffee and I admired her from the recess. She was such a contradiction, ultramodern and assertive but a very traditional relationship with her family. I wondered if she'd ever been subjected to racialism, she was so smiley and nice looking I doubted it, but what did I know? I vaguely remembered some anti-Ugandan Asian demonstrations a few years ago, it was Enoch Powell, or someone like him.

'At least it's freshly brewed, possibly a bit weak, though,' as she put the coffee down.

'Until I went to uni, I thought Nescafe and Maxwell House were the coffee alternatives,' I said. I poured the cold milk in my coffee. I looked up to see Anita looking a bit serious.

'Frank, I need to say something you might not want to hear.' My heart sank, as I put down the milk.

'I've really enjoyed today and the other times we've been out…'

'But?' I interrupted. I could see she was tense, I went to hold her arm, but she moved it away.

'I'm apparently getting engaged to a pharmacist back home in Leicester next month and wanted you to know.' I stared close-mouthed at the news.

'Well, I didn't see that coming.' She carried on quickly, 'He's a family friend, it's been settled for years that we would. I'm not expecting you to understand, you don't get Asian families.'

'Phew. Bugger,' I said, 'I'm lost for words. Bugger.'

'I know, that's why I'm stopping now before I do something I'll regret.' I looked closely at her, was it really some kind of arranged marriage in 1979 for God's sake? I said nothing though. We drank our coffee in silence.

As we drove towards Gateacre still in silence, I glanced over at Anita, but she was just staring straight ahead. She parked by the bins near the flat, and I put one hand on the door to get out. I turned to face her and said, 'I feel a bit disappointed, but

I'm not up for arguing with you. But would you do one thing for me before we split?'

'What?' she said

'Could I have one proper kiss before we split?'

She looked ahead, thinking for a moment and said, 'Yes,' turning towards me.

'No, I mean outside the car.'

'Ok.'

We got out and as I went round to her side of the car, she smoothed her skirt down.

I moved her hair away from her eyes, held her face and gave her a long deep kiss. After what seemed an age, she withdrew but not before I felt like her body had melded into mine. She blinked, breathed heavily and lent back against the car. Her eyes were wide open, like a cat.

'Now you know why I can't see you,' as she turned away closed the door and drove slowly off. I stood watching her go, but she didn't look back. I looked up at my grotty flat on the first floor walked past it and down the road to the Black Bull.

— **14** —

Hypo

I'd agreed, ages ago, to help the white-collar staff personnel people with some interviewing for comptometer operators. I knew they worked in a first-floor office with fifty or so women with some weird mechanical adding machine doing payroll and the like. Any unknown young man walking through there was wolf-whistled, which was embarrassing, if a one-off, experience for me. My fellow interviewer was a fifty-plus-year-old blonde called Lil, who was the 'Manageress' in charge of 'her girls'. I had read through the job description and experience required but was puzzled by the vagueness of the academic qualifications required. I asked Lil about them.

'I like about four or five O levels including maths, but no A levels as that makes them unsuitable,' she said.

'Why's that?' I asked.

'It's a very routine job with no promotion prospects and only one manageress and that's me,' she emphasised.

'Are there any section heads or supervisor type jobs at all? I said.

'No. It's a very flat structure, the sixty-three girls and me.'

'Oh.'

'Anyway, in Detroit, they've started to replace the girls there with electronic computers, so I don't think we'll be here much longer.'

'Oh, really?'

'The problem they have to sort is how the computers keep paper records for audit, but they're working on it.'

Bill suddenly appeared with Anita in tow, the first time I'd seen her since our relationship had cooled yet again. I looked away for a second, and then back.

'Lil, I'm afraid Frank is needed for an urgent meeting on a drillings manning issue, Anita here will take over his interviewing duties.'

I stood and gave the application forms to Anita, focusing on her nose so I didn't have to see those eyes.

'There you go, four O levels max, no party animals, skirts must be worn.'

Anita and Bill laughed but Lil said angrily,

'I never said that.'

Bill briefed me on our way back to the piggeries, but I wasn't listening as it had been aching to hear Anita laugh. I should toughen up, after two dates for God's sake. I went into Bill's office for a briefing when Bill's office phone rang.

'Right, you'll have to forget that meeting for the time being, there's a forklift truck driver who's just had an epileptic fit and driven his truck over the container bay in the knock down area. You'll have to go, there's no one else.'

I sighed, picked up my pad and walked quickly to the Complete Knock Down (CKD) area where car kits were exported. The site ambulance was just pulling away, but I could see the truck on its side on the bay beneath one of the dozen or so container loading bays. Dr Abbot was there and the forklift driver was already in the ambulance, ready to go to hospital. It was a serious incident and the atmosphere was tense. The foreman was shooing the shocked staff back to their jobs with a 'the show's over lads, back to work.' The superintendent called us into his nearby office for a debrief.

Dr Abbot spoke first,

'He'll probably be ok, he may have a couple of broken ribs and possibly concussion.'

I spoke next,

'I didn't realise we employed epileptics on jobs like these…'

'We don't and he was not epileptic; it was a hypo episode.'

'So, he was diabetic do you mean?' I said.

'Yes,' said the medic, but obviously embarrassed by the situation.

The foreman, who was sweating profusely explained,

'We didn't know that he's never said anything to me. He's only been with us six months.'

'I thought FLT driver jobs were agreed progression jobs for line operators from the production lines,' I said.

'They normally are,' said the superintendent. 'But we occasionally take people with experience direct from outside when we have no one trained in the bank; he was one of those.'

We went our separate ways and I walked back with Dr Abbott towards our offices near the front of the factory. The container area was already roped off awaiting a factory inspector.

'If he joined six months ago, wouldn't he have a medical that would have picked up the diabetes?' I said.

The doctor looked daggers at me as we walked along.

'It's a new company policy that we only do medical self questionnaires now, so unless someone says they have an issue that needs to be followed up we don't routinely examine everyone before they start work. It's my view that he won't have ticked that box on his form, because he knew we wouldn't take him on if he did.'

'Ok. Will his medical questionnaire be in his personnel file? I asked, surprised at the news on changes to the pre-employment medicals.

'Yes, but we have a copy too. Come over in five minutes and we'll look at his file together.'

I called into Bill's office to update him. He hardly looked up but said,

'Check his file by all means but when he returns, sack him for lying on his application form. Or, if he has just developed it, you'll have to sack him anyway as he can't drive an FLT anymore.'

I listened and didn't argue with Bill but went back to my office and sat down puzzling over the issue. I heard a tapping and looked up to see Anita doing a coffee sign, I shook my head and concentrated on the report. I felt a bit too raw to be looking at Anita across a desk at the moment. I went over to the medical centre where Dr Abbot already had the file out. 'I've just spoken to his GP. He developed type two diabetes about three years ago and it's normally well controlled but, as I suspected, he didn't mention any of this on his questionnaire when he joined.'

Before I could mention Bill's clear view of the action needed, Dr Abbot looked at me and said,

'Frank, I know from the flag burner episode you're the rare exception in personnel, a sentient being.'

'Well, I'm not sure many would agree with that...'

'The point is, it's the easiest thing in the world to dismiss him for falsifying his application form or whatever you would call it in personnelese.'

'Go on.'

'By sacking him we're just driving the problem underground. The fact is that epileptics, diabetics, the handicapped, all cover things up or they know they will never work again. Why can't we employ him where he is not driving and is not a lone worker? I guarantee he would be fine.'

I thought about it for a moment. The guy's personnel record as an employee was first class.

'Well, there are plenty of jobs like that in the factory, but are we not then just rewarding him for lying to us?'

'We'd all do the same in his situation.'

I looked up at the doctor, the one who had gone out on a limb to help me with the POW flag burner case. My thoughts crystallised in an instant. I knew I'd ignore Bill's instruction and that I might come to regret it in the cold light of day.

My frustration with company management on the drillings issue, combined with the Anita brush off and my slightly depressing life were also drivers. Sod it.

'Ok, ok. Senior management will go apeshit, as Jim would say. But yes, yes, I'll try and arrange for him to be redeployed into a non-machinery job rather than be dismissed. I'll do my best to arrange it, I suspect the unions will violently oppose it as well as management though.'

Not particularly wanting to go back to my claustrophobic office, I stopped at one of the line workers' tea rooms for a brew. The room was empty, just a twenty square foot partitioned space with a few tables and the inevitable Klix machine. I noticed a kettle as well, as the Klix stuff was powdered tea someone else must think it undrinkable I thought. I left the door open and stared at the spot welders in subassembly, making parts on job and finish that would eventually end up on the production line. I absorbed the smells, flashes, noise, and the shouts of the operators. For a while I found it oddly relaxing. I headed back eventually, as I would need to sort the accident situation out. I found Willie John having a smoke and tea in my office.

'Aye aye, the wanderer returns. I would get ye a tea, but I heard you just had one in my members' tearoom,' just to let me know he knew everything.

'I'm no representing the FLT lad, the local steward can do it. I just wanted you to know, if you'd used progression and no appointed from outside, ye would nae be jeopardising my members' lives.'

'What's your view of what the disciplinary should be then?' I queried.

'I heard the factory inspector may be prosecuting yon company for even allowin' him in the job mind, so I'm expectin' the sack. You should nae be cutting back on proper medicals to save a few pennies, ye put my members at risk.' I thought quickly about the merits of sharing what I was thinking with him and decided to take the plunge.

'Well, it may surprise you to know that I'm thinking of redeploying him into a clerical job in a shop floor office.'

'Ye are not,' spitting out his tea and wiping himself. 'They're a progression job too, and they're few and far between. We will nae stand in the way of his dismissal.'

'But if we redeploy him, we can then offer his FLT driving job to a line worker, rather than go outside.'

'Is the man a relative of yours or did ye lose at cards to him?' Willie John exclaimed.

'I have never laid eyes on the man,' I said deadpan.

'Then you're soft in the head, or there's some trickery at work.' He got up to go.

'I just want you to be neutral if push comes to shove with production management that's all. You know you owe me that.' He looked at me long and hard.

'Aye, well I'll think about it,' shook his head and walked out.

I agonised over whether to talk it through with Bill, and decided it was such an important change I couldn't get away with my normal 'do it and ask forgiveness afterwards' approach. I reluctantly went to see him to explain what Dr Abbot and I were thinking. Bill dismissed my argument after giving me a fair hearing, mainly because he saw the principle of lying on the application form as sacrosanct and not negotiable. I was brassed off but knew taking on management and the unions together might be a bridge too far, even for me. I rang the doctor to give him the bad news. I was surprised to hear he wasn't disheartened; he said the UK Occupational Health Committee was about to recommend more rights for handicapped people in employment situations, a bit like the Rehabilitation of Offenders Act for criminals passed in 1974. He would demand a meeting with Eric which was his right as the site senior medical officer. I said nothing; it sounded like big trouble.

Thirty minutes later, Bill burst into my office more annoyed than I'd seen him for ages.

'You're lucky I don't take your challenges personally, you maverick. Abbott has demanded to see Eric and requested your presence at the meeting. Eric wants to know why I haven't briefed him and don't know what's going on.'

'I just told him the result of our discussion, I'm not responsible for what he does next am I?' I said defensively.

'Well, the meeting is 4 p.m. Eric's office tomorrow, and I'm still not supporting your view in case you're still in any doubt.'

He raised his eyebrows and left. I felt a little embarrassed; Bill was a great boss and he'd a lot to teach me, and he did well in keeping an even keel in the maelstrom of day-to-day labour relations. I went to get a coffee, to find Tim and Anita chatting by the machine. Tim tried to draw me into their conversation about the Beatles *White Album*, but I declined. I was a bit sharper than I meant to be.

Five minutes later, Anita opened my door and stood there, arms folded. 'I know you might not feel like talking to me, but that's no excuse to be rude to your colleagues.' She shut the door behind her before I could reply. I was embarrassed to think she was probably right. I decided I'd had enough of it all for one day, took my papers and decided I would revise the FLT arguments at home. I stopped in Tim's office on the way to the car park.

'Just came in to apologise for being short earlier, I'm sorry.'

'Ok old chap, I know you have a lot on,' in his lovely colonial brogue.

'One thing though, that might relate to your FLT case.' It didn't surprise me that the whole world would know of the incident by now, probably through the unions. 'My brother was epileptic as a teenager. He seemed to grow out of it later so it's not a problem anymore. The thing is, whenever he answered "yes" in post job offer medicals, he never got the job. The job offer was usually conditional on passing the medical. Of course, now he always says "no". Just thought you might like to use him as a case if you need to.'

I thanked Tim and said I would raise it when I got a chance tomorrow. When I got home, I prepared my case on the Formica table under the kitchen fluorescent light. I felt a bit down about the harsh company response to the case, then there was Anita, and my whole unfulfilling life. I went to bed with a cup of tea, thinking at least I had five index cards with arguments for change for the meeting tomorrow.

The only person I had not considered might be at the meeting was the site safety manager. Eric, Bill, Dr Abbot and I were the others present. Dr Abbot made an impassioned plea for a change in policy, quoting the BMA and various occupational evidence to suggest that legal protection for nondisclosure would soon be the law. The safety manager, Peter, had Head Office's legal view that the company was vicariously liable for allowing a diabetic to drive the truck, but it was Eric that put the nail in the coffin. He said that lying on the application form on medical issues was no different than educational qualifications or criminal history. If we gave way on this, we would set a custom and precedent.

I gave my view about how the system encouraged prospective employees to lie and put other employees at risk, quoting Tim's brother in evidence.

After going round in circles Eric, to his credit, surprised me by concluding that the case for change did have some merit. It was agreed for the future, that if an employee developed a disability like epilepsy or diabetes, they should be redeployed in the first instance rather than dismissed. However, anyone lying on their application form when they started should still be dismissed. He added that a careful re-examination of the problem of not giving all new staff a medical should be looked at as a matter of urgency. Bill stayed behind and I walked back with the doctor.

I said, 'I'll give him a one-off special reference to explain how he came to leave us, something like that if he avoids lone worker jobs, he would be a good employee. I shouldn't do it, but I will give my name and phone number in case I get a follow up call. I thought you made a great case.'

'Thanks for your support. Well at least we have a significant policy change and I can also now go back to proper medicals and tell Head Office where they can stick their cost cutting questionnaires.' He insisted on shaking hands with me before we walked our separate ways.

The dismissal was done the following afternoon. His injuries were not that bad after all, there was perfunctorily representation of his case by the steward. He admitted lying to get the job, and at the end of it I said, 'I would like to see Mr Warburton in my office for five minutes before he leaves.' This caused some consternation amongst senior management and the steward, who left at once.

'It's effective immediately,' said the superintendent.

'I'll escort him to the security lodge myself if that makes you happier,' I said.

Warburton followed me to my office, puzzled, and I sat him down.

'Sometimes things happen in organisations that are right for them but not for the individual.' I realised I sounded patronising. 'One or two of us think it's a shame you are leaving like this. You need to think seriously about what you apply for in future; you could have done yourself or others a serious…'

Willie John burst through the door.

'You can't talk to my members without a fuckin' steward present…'

'He's not your member anymore, he's been sacked so bugger off out of my office…'

He ignored me and pointed to Warburton.

'Are ye happy here on ye own?' Warburton looked from one to the other and weakly said, 'Yes.'

Willie John gave me a hard stare and left, slamming the door behind himself. I noticed Anita from one side and Tim from the other peer through the glass partitions.

'As I was saying. You need to avoid driving and lone worker type jobs, ok?

He nodded.

'I've prepared this reference saying you've been an excellent worker and have said you left for personal reasons. Anyone in a personnel department who wants to know more can ring me on my number. It will be on company letterhead, so please only show it to prospective employers otherwise I'll be in trouble. And if Willie John or any steward wants to know what we discussed tell them nothing, they've been absolutely bloody useless in their support for you.'

Warburton thanked me, still in a bit of a daze and with what looked like ribs bandaged up under his shirt. I escorted him to the security lodge, shook hands and left. I wondered on the way back to my office whether Willie John would make a formal complaint, either about me seeing Warburton after the meeting unaccompanied or our contretemps. I realised I was so fed up with the job that I didn't give a toss either way. I was so angry with the unions for being so bloody conservative and reactionary on issues like this and management for acting like bloody robots.

— **15** —

Election

In the last general election, I'd campaigned for the Labour MP in Lancaster, where I was a student. I left work, intending to drive the 120-mile round trip to vote, as I was still registered to vote there. After only a few miles, I turned round and drove home.

It was not ideological, my volte face was due entirely to the behaviour of the unions, the flying pickets, tanker drivers, gravediggers, and kangaroo courts for staff refusing to join unions. I remembered shouting as a teenager, 'Thatcher, Thatcher, milk snatcher,' over the loss of my third of a pint of free school milk. Maybe that was why I was not keen on her as a leader. I knew she'd been 20% behind in popularity versus Labour's Jim Callaghan when she'd been appointed party leader, but that had reduced as he'd turned out to be such a weak leader himself. The economy, the cost of living – he was a complete no mark. I remembered Tim had said he might be voting Liberal, but what had they done in the two 1974 elections but propped up a weak Labour government? A 'bit of a wasted vote,' I had remarked to Tim, who insisted that the Liberals had been a good influence on local councils, although even he was perplexed by the Jeremy Thorpe dog shooting saga.

After putting my car battery on charge, I made up some Smash and heated up some mushy peas and a tinned pie. I fell asleep at seven and woke up at two in the morning, when the results were starting to come through. I was totally shocked to see one of the first results was Dagenham, and that it had swung 13% to Thatcher. The Liberal vote was being destroyed and the new TV voter swing tool was predicting a 50 seat Tory majority. No way!

At 4 a.m. Callaghan was pictured in his 1950s Rover going somewhere. I made a cheese and piccalilli sandwich; commentators were saying their predictions were way out and one said it spelled the end of high-spending Keynes policies and the start of low inflation monetarism. I waited, glued to the screen in utter disbelief, and listened to Thatcher's acceptance speech,

'Where there is discord may we bring harmony, where there is despair may we bring hope.' A bit religious but a good sentiment, nevertheless.

I fell asleep again and was woken at 8 a.m. by my friend Pete, who rang to verbally abuse me for voting Tory, not that I had voted. We agreed to meet that evening to discuss the result. I put on 'Hanging on the Telephone' by Blondie, a band I'd seen at university before they were famous, when I was a bouncer at the university concert hall. It always cheered me up; then the real phone rang, and it was Bill, 'You know that job Jim mentioned a while ago, well it's going down tomorrow lunchtime'.

'What job? Anyway, you know I've booked today off as holiday as I've been up all night watching the election…'

'That's why I'm ringing. It's a PTA plant senior steward, a right militant apparently, skiving off at the Red Lion every Friday drinking and doing the horses.'

'Why isn't it a PTA personnel job? I said, not wanting to go in at all.

'Because he knows them all, but he doesn't know you and Anita. You both really need to be there two o'clock onwards tomorrow.'

'No, I can't do it with Anita…'

'Funny, that's what she just said about you. You were as thick as thieves. I guess you've fallen out?'

After a short pause, Bill continued,

'Look, Tim is in Ceylon, the steward would definitely recognise Jim and me so that leaves you and Anita. The PTA personnel guys will confront and suspend him; you two are just witnesses, maybe taking a photo that's all. Come on, man. Be at the Adelphi Hotel for a planning meeting 9.30 a.m. A boy and his best bird are right inconspicuous.' Reluctantly, I agreed.

'Ok then, but why the Adelphi?' I asked; it was an expensive city centre hotel.

'It's a kind of secret ops room off site, secure. It's Room 101, be there or be square!' We discussed our mutual amazement at the election result and then Bill rang off, without mentioning any complaint from the convenor about the Warburton meeting.

I considered ringing Anita to see if she knew any more, and it made sense to give her a lift as it was in the city. I decided I would ring.

'Bill, thank god…'

'Sorry to disappoint you, it's Frank.'

'Oh, well great anyway. I was going to ring you if Bill didn't ring me back, I'm really worried about this job.'

'Because it's with me,' I said before I could stop myself.

'Fuck off, Frank. This is serious, it's apparently a rough council estate drinking den.'

'And?'

'How do we know we won't get beaten up or robbed or glassed or something?'

'Well, Bill won't be at home, he said he was off to the theatre in Chester after he rang me, so you can't ask him anything.'

'Well what clothes do I need for instance?'

'What do you mean?' I said, surprised by the question, but then beginning to understand as Anita was always expensively dressed.

'Ok. You probably need to be dressed down, a bit tarty, not student dress down mind.' I couldn't stop myself from laughing at what I imagined Anita's face would look like.

'It's not funny Frank. Won't they notice an Asian girl, and what happens if it's a Paki-bashing pub? I've never been in a place like that, even at college.'

I finally picked up on her worried tone, and realised it wasn't about me being there but a deeper worry about being safe.

'Ok look, we're just witnessing a steward being caught for boozing and gambling in company time, we're just witnesses in case he denies it, that's all,' I said as calmly as I could.

'It could still go horribly wrong, there might be an army of skinheads and football hooligans…'

'Anita, pack it in, it's not some episode out of *The Sweeney*, and it's a bloody crap pub within walking distance of the factory.'

'It's all very last minute…'

'I agree with you there, I'm supposed to be on a day's holiday today, sleeping off the election,' I said as jauntily as I could manage. 'Listen, I'll pick you up at nine o'clock, we'll go in my car as it's less likely to get nicked.'

'Yeah, ho ho,' she said sounding slightly happier.

'Now stop worrying, and I'll see you soon.' I rang Pete to rearrange our drink as sleep was going to be a higher priority. I was still brassed off with Anita and her supposed partner, but maybe working together on a job would improve things at the professional level at least. Anyway, anything that was not the drillings dispute would be light relief at the moment.

I picked her up at her flat in leafy Aigburth, a nice Victorian conversion near the park. I glanced at her clothes, looked like normal business ones to me but I thought better of mentioning it. I'd put on casual clothes, like I was going for a pint in my local.

'What are these?' said Anita, looking at my two red furry dice hanging down from the mirror.

'Oh, they stop kids nicking the car as they think it must be owned by a drug dealer,' I said half seriously.

'It would have to be a pretty unsuccessful drug dealer,' and she half smiled, sitting there with her arms crossed.

'Maybe an apprentice drug dealer then. I can leave it unlocked, no one will be seen dead in this.' Ten minutes later, we were parking among the Granadas and Capris in the Adelphi car park.

'A tea leaf's paradise,' I said, looking at the smart cars. 'I think I might need to get a vinyl roof fitted.' Reception directed us to the right conference room, we knocked and went in. I was bowled over; there were flipcharts, white boards, 35mm film projectors – it was like a crime scene investigation room. The Senior PO, Tom Brady, introduced us to the others; he was immaculately dressed like a fashion model, strange for a would-be personnel manager. There were at least four other people I vaguely recognised as fellow blue-collar staff personnel officers.

'Real thanks for helping us out today, and I know it's short notice, but we've been planning for weeks and security is all. We have to nail this bastard.' They outlined the plan. The steward was deputy convenor and the man behind a lot of the militancy in the paint shop in their view. He never did a day's work and they knew he drank a skinful every Friday in the Red Lion, staying till around 4 p.m. Tom and a colleague would approach him in the pub about 3 p.m. and suspend him for a disciplinary the following Monday. They expected a senior union district official to be involved and were planning for an Industrial Tribunal.

'You two just have lunch like boyfriend/girlfriend and we have a special little camera here for you take some pictures.'

Anita immediately said, 'Why?'

'If he tries to deny being there or legs it away, we'll have the pictures to prove it. Before you ask, it's a special Minolta spy camera from Head Office, really small and easily concealed and used.'

He then looked at Anita, his gaze lasting just too long.

'Here's fifty quid, would you go out and get some better clothes for a Speke pub? I need the receipt, but you can keep them. Just turn left out of the hotel, loads of shops.' Anita glanced at me with apprehension, but she picked up her bag and left.

'By the way Frank, our dry run lads say scampi and chips in the basket is the only edible thing there.'

I smiled, why was I not surprised?

'I hear from Bill that your car will blend in well parked near the pub?'

'You could say that, but it's got new tyres so if it's up on bricks when I come out you can buy me some new ones!' Everyone laughed with me.

'This is a serious amount of effort, plans of the pub, dry runs...' I said.

'He's cost us thousands of cars and is trying to overthrow the more moderate convenor,' Tom replied.

'How many other people will there be in the pub, do you reckon?' I said.

'About six to ten max from our dry run.'

Anita soon arrived back and went to the 'Ladies' powder room' to change. Someone from the back of the room whistled, and I turned round. I stared goggle-eyed, Anita was dressed in a short, tight black leather skirt, a skin-tight diaphanous white blouse, and the biggest pair of wedge shoes I'd ever seen.

She did a flirtatious twirl, everyone stared.

'So, do I look the part then?'

Tom was the first to speak,

'You look like a scouse scrubber or a page three model, not sure which!' Everyone clapped. After a while it was time to go, so I put on my best scouse accent, 'Come ahead la, we need to moove.' We tottered out to the car, Anita smoothing down her short skirt before she got in. She glanced up to see me staring at her thighs.

'Stop leering, Frank and keep your eyes on the road.'

I couldn't stop grinning as we drove back to Speke.

'What?' said Anita.

'Oh, nothing,' I thought it took some balls to get dressed like that, like she was an actress or something. At least, I thought, her irrational fear seemed to have evaporated.

'We've got five minutes before we go in, is there anything you want to run over?'

'No, now I'm dressed like this, I feel I'm playing a part. It's not really me but it's a strange bloody job we've got, isn't it? My mum would be really cross.' I put on my Harrington jacket, opened a couple more buttons on the shirt and got out of the car. I was surprised at how nice the pub building was, it was like you would see in Soho in London. We walked in. I took Anita's arm and she didn't resist but glanced at me. It was surprisingly dark and the walls were covered with both Liverpool and Everton football stuff, which I'd never seen before as it was normally one or the other.

The barmaid was peroxide blonde, skinny and looked seventy at least.

'Err, a pint of mild, a barley wine, err half a shandy and a Pepsi luv,' I said. 'And two scampi and chips as well, like.' I noticed some of the regulars turn round to look at us. I paid and we walked slowly over to two seats from where we could see the other end of the bar, where the steward sat, watching the racing on TV in silent mode with his left hand on the pub bar telephone, presumably ready to phone in a bet

'Turn round a bit and move your legs out of the way so I can take some shots under the table,' I whispered.

'Bugger,' I continued. The camera shutter had made a loud clicking that it had not made in the hotel, and an elderly couple turned round to stare.

The scampi and chips arrived, and Anita pushed hers round the plate while I tucked in, all the time watching the steward.

'I'll stink of smoke and vinegar when we leave here,' she whispered. I reassured her that she was acting pretty cool given how nervous she'd been about the whole set up earlier.

Suddenly, from the left I saw Tom and a colleague walk in, approach the steward and start talking to him. Voices were raised, there was a muffled argument for a minute or so and I leaned under the table and took three pictures with the shutter click echoing in the pub.

'Shit' I said.

The personnel people eventually left, but the barmaid started to point at us, and the other customers turned round to stare as well.

'I think it's time to go,' I said.' Anita had heard the commotion but had deliberately not turned round and didn't see what was going on. As we stood up and walked towards the door, we saw the barmaid point at us and say, 'Wait yuh hurry. That's them Steve,' and a small muscley man of about forty appeared in front of us and stood in our way, with his arms crossed.

'What's you're fuckin' game eh, taking pictures eh?'

'None of your business what I do with me best tart,' I said aggressively.

The barman looked disdainfully at Anita. 'Just her was it, or are you with those company gaffers causin' trouble in my pub, eh?'

I took Anita firmly by the arm and pushed towards the man, who was still blocking the way.

'Piss of out of it before I smack yuh,' I said snarling. He moved aside.

'You're a fuckin' company nark you are, I can smell you… Gail, ring our Tel and get him round 'ere now.'

We pushed past him quickly and I turned round and gave him a V sign.

Safe in the car, Anita was shaking and ashen-faced, and I was trembling from the adrenalin rush the near fight. I smiled weakly, praying the car would start. It did. We drove off as an Escort van skidded to a halt beside the pub with a gorilla-like bloke driving. Anita was staring straight ahead in shock.

'Phew, that was a close one,' I said, exhaling deeply and glancing in the rear mirror. 'They don't seem to be following anyway. Are you ok?'

'No,' was the stark response.

'We need to go back to the Adelphi to drop off the camera and do a debrief,' I said looking at Anita.

'Just drop me off at my flat, I want to get out of these clothes and ring my mum. You can do it without me.'

Given her tone, I did as I was asked. When we got to her flat, Anita took the bag of her normal clothes off the rear seat, opened the door, said thanks and left.

That went well then, I said to myself driving off.

Back at the Adelphi, one of the POs went off to develop the photos while I was debriefed. They were all pleased with the result, till they got to the report of the clicking noise, the barmaid and the confrontation. They were riveted by my story.

The Senior PO, Tom, asked me if I thought the steward would recognise us if he saw us again and I said I was pretty sure he would, especially with an Asian girlfriend. A little later the developed pictures came back; a Scottish PO called Niall handed the seven shots around the group.

'Wow, these two are not so relevant...'

I looked at the two under-the table pictures and blushed, as they were mostly of Anita's thighs. Tom laughed and said,

'Ok guys let's get packed up, the disciplinary hearing is on Monday. Frank, I'll let you know whether he denies being there or not. If the former, we'll have to use you in evidence, but given the landlord incident I'll try and avoid that. Thanks again and for Anita, remind her I need the receipt for her clothes.'

I drove home shattered, probably because of the adrenalin of the aggressive response with the landlord and not sleeping on election night. I still wanted to see the latest on the new government but couldn't summon the energy and went straight to bed. I went out early Saturday and came back with five newspapers to read their analysis of the significance of the election. I laid them out on the kitchen table. It looked to me like the 'wet' Jim Prior and 'dry' Keith Joseph would soon become well known in the personnel community. Prior was consulting on introducing curbs on secondary picketing and blacking non-union workers. Joseph had announced that shipbuilding and aerospace would be privatised very soon, and that insurance, banking, road haulage and pharmaceuticals were all off the agenda for any state interference whatsoever. I wondered if the stop stewards would feel guilty on Monday, as they had effectively destroyed the Labour government. But the Tory share of the vote was still only 44%, even though they had won over some National Front voters who liked the tougher Thatcher view of immigration. It seemed to be the Midlands and new towns, the skilled working class, the fitters and electricians, that had voted Tory; there was not a great change in Liverpool with its Labour vote.

My phone rang.

'Frank, it's me.'

Hearing Anita's voice cheered me up,

'Oh hi, I guess you want to hear what happened at the Adelphi then? I said.

'Yes and no.'

'Oh.'

'I've had a really shit weekend at home because of what happened in the pub and I need to talk to someone who understands – that leaves a field of one.'

'What me?' I said surprised.

'Yeah, can we meet for a pub lunch or something if you're free?'

'Sure,' I said.

'But not that pub where my car wheels got stolen...' she laughed,

'Ok. Better be the Childe again then, let's say in about an hour – see you at one o'clock.'

I was puzzled, as it was only recently that she'd said she didn't want to see me again and if it was about the pub episode, we could have done it at work on Monday? I knew she felt the incident was unpleasant, but it wasn't that big a deal in the grander scheme of things? I had an uncomfortable feeling I was missing something again but shook my head and got back to the election newspapers.

Anita arrived in her smart camel hair coat and smiled, 'Hi there,' happier than the last time we met when I had dropped her off at home.

'How are you?'

'Great. How did you get on at the Adelphi then?'

After I had got a round in and the menus, I explained the wrap up meeting result and the emerging view that because of the landlord incident they would do their best not to use us as witnesses at all.

'So, we wasted our time then, put ourselves in danger for absolutely nothing?'

'Well, I wouldn't say that, but it's a shame that the camera sound was so loud and attracted the barmaid's attention.'

The waitress appeared so I stopped while she took our orders.

'I was so upset by Friday that I drove home to Leicester to see my family. I made the mistake of telling my mum about the clothes I had to wear, and I got a full lecture on quitting my job after wearing "tramp's clothes" …'

I laughed again.

'It's not bloody funny. My mum then invited the family of the boy who they've planned to marry me round and they told me to give up my job, get married, and live above the pharmacy his dad's just bought for him.'

I paused mid-drink.

'You are joking…'

'I'm not. I lost my temper, shouting that no one had consulted me about my career and who I was going to marry, and it led to a big row, with no one talking to me in my family at all.'

'Well, that might be ok in East Bengal or whatever, but not 1978 great bloody Britain…'

Her eyes rolled upwards,

'I don't expect you to get Asian families but it's all I've got…'

'Ok, ok.' I said as the food arrived.

I was trying to process what I had just heard while eating when Anita calmly said, 'By the way, thanks for getting us out in one piece, I was probably too upset on Friday to say so.'

'Yeah, even I could see that.'

'Frank, I can see now I should have told you why I was upset by the Red Lion incident blowing up but it's personal. Maybe I've had a sheltered upbringing, but we had a traumatic incident on the school bus when I was with my elder brother. He was beaten up by skinheads who got on the bus "Paki bashing" and a similar thing had also happened to him in a local pub which he covered up. Ever since then I've had panic attacks in strange pubs and buses, I know it's stupid but there it is, I can't help what I feel.'

'Anita – I'm so sorry, that's a horrible thing to have happened. I don't know what to say, bloody hell.'

We moved on rather than dwelled on it, and spent the next hour laughing about the absurdity of the election and what impact it may have on our jobs.

The following Monday, I had the two black and white pictures of Anita's legs on the Formica table in front of me over breakfast. I was in two minds whether to keep them or give them to Anita. I thought they made her look like a glamorous fashion model like you might see in the *Sunday Times* magazine, but she might not see it that way. Nor might her ex-fiancé if he ever was.

The Monday following the election, I was first in and, after checking the factory was working, I sat down to look at my diary. Anita knocked and came in, holding two coffees.

Before she could say anything there was another quick knock on the door and Bill waltzed in fag in mouth, double-breasted suit jacket open.

'Morning both. I've just heard from the PTA how your successful your sting was. Looks like they feel they have him bang to rights.'

'Didn't they tell you what happened to us in the pub, then?' I said.

'Yeah, but you were only an insurance policy if he denied being there and, it appears, he hasn't, so it looks like you'll not be needed further. Oh, don't forget the clothes receipt Anita, and I was told you need to show me the glam pics of Anita, Frank?' I was caught off-guard and went puce.

'Umm, yeah, yeah, Tom gave me a couple of the photos I took.' I saw Anita's eyes narrow, and lips purse.

'You didn't mention any pictures of me, when do I get to see them?'

'They must be at home, I'll bring them in tomorrow.'

— **16** —

Cottaging

I was in Anita's office having a coffee when Bill marched in.

'Morning you two. Something happened at the weekend concerning one of your managers Anita.'

'I'm happy to leave, Bill,' I said.

'No stay, Anita might want some assistance with this one.' Anita and I looked at each other, puzzled. Bill sat down on the spare chair, flicking off cigarette ash.

'One of your foremen has been caught cottaging in Chester.'

After a short pause, Anita and I said almost together, 'What's that?'

'Importuning,' said Bill.

'And what's that?' I said.

'You know, like Oscar Wilde. Apparently, your guy was caught with his privates through a hole in the wall in the public toilets down on the riverside in Chester.'

There was a stunned silence from Anita. Bill smiled, 'He's been released on bail. It's Anita's patch but I thought it was a bit rum asking a woman to deal with it, that's all.' Anita quickly said, 'I can handle it.'

I burst out laughing, but no one else got the humour. Bill continued, 'It's an inside tip through public affairs, we don't have the details yet but if I can leave it with you.' Bill got up and left.

I looked at Anita, and laughed,

'*News of the World* stuff, I guess. I'll bet even Jim won't have seen a case like this.' Anita got up looking thoughtful,

'I'll do some research and bounce it off you this afternoon,' she said.

I put my portable transistor on for the 1 p.m. news, but nothing much seemed to have happened on the Westminster front to my disappointment. I bought a ham sandwich and returned to my desk to do some research on the cottaging case. I looked up 'Croner's' which was a bit of a personnel bible for employment law and had good case histories. It was not much help as there were no cases, so I started by looking up 'importuning' in the dictionary:

'Importuning is making sexual advances by offering services as a prostitute, but one can also importune a waiter for profiteroles.' I burst out laughing.

Next, I looked up 'cottaging:'

'Performing homosexual acts in a public toilet, derived from the Victorian era.'

Ten minutes later Anita burst through the door without knocking, 'That bitch!'

I was startled, but secretly relieved it couldn't be me that had upset her.

'You wouldn't believe what she just said to me.'

'Who?'

'The plant manager's secretary Julie just said to me,' and imitated her snooty voice, '"I'm surprised to see a professional woman at work in trousers."'

'Really? Does she prefer knickers then?' I joked, lost on Anita in her rage.

'"I don't allow my secretaries to wear trousers" to which I naturally said, "I'm not one of your secretaries."'

'Good on you,' I said trying to think which other women at work did wear trousers.

'Bloody queen bee,' said Anita, and sat down. After a few more minutes of letting off steam we were able to move to her office to discuss the case. I liked Anita's office, it was as grotty as mine but had three grand aspidistra potted plants desperately trying to survive in no natural light. It was sexist to think it,

152

but it was a shit office compared with the daylighted, smart offices the more junior female personnel administrators had in the main block. Anita sat down with her huge whiteboard and multicoloured pens and led the discussion.

'We know he hasn't been charged yet but there's no way of getting more info. I can't find out anything, whether the other person was over the age of consent, whether a sexual assault actually took place or even if it was a police trap. So, for me there's no question of suspending him, which is what I thought Bill was implying we should do.'

'Absolutely agree,' I said. 'If it's flaky information from some person in the police force who owes Ford PR a favour, we should keep our heads down until we hear officially. Even if charged, unless he's convicted of something, we should do nothing.'

'Thanks,' said Anita. 'I'll tell Bill our views.'

'Do you want me to come as well?' I asked.

'No, I think I can handle this one,' and she went to look for Bill. After she'd gone, I thought I would say to Anita that maybe she was right about that Friday in the Red Lion. With the benefit of hindsight, there had been more risk to both of us than we had anticipated. If any other odd jobs like that came up again, I should ask a lot more questions up front.

That evening, I was watching the 9 p.m. BBC news on the election when Bill rang me at home.

'Frank, the PTA steward was dismissed today, the appeal is with the District Official and their IRM this week. It sounds like his defence is that he returned for his reading glasses which he'd left there. So, he's not denying being in the pub, which means there's no need to involve you or Anita. Just thought you should be the first to know.'

'Ok, thanks Bill.' I thought about ringing Anita, but no doubt Bill would have done so, so we could discuss anything relevant at work tomorrow.

I nodded at Anita when she arrived in the office and looked through the glass partition to where I had left the envelope in the middle of her desk. Still standing, she opened it to find the two large black and white photos with my 'there are no copies' note. She looked up, saw me and did a thumbs up sign. I poked my head round her door,

'Good morning, did Bill give you the good news last night?'

'Yes thanks, it's a relief to me that we won't be called,' said Anita sitting down.

'And what did you think of the pictures? I'm not sure your future fiancé would like me keeping them so they're yours,' I said.

'Well, you know what, I won't be asking his opinion.'

I was completely taken aback, but decided to change the topic while the remark sank in.

'Well, it's probably a good thing we won't be called anyway,' I said.

Anita stared at me for a moment.

'What?' I said alarmed.

'Oh, nothing. I need to prepare for a nine o' clock interview,' and began to get up from her chair. She left and I wasn't even sure if she was keeping or destroying the photos from what little she'd said, we really were not on the same wavelength sometimes, I thought.

— **17** —

Expenses

One afternoon, Bill called the POs into a special meeting, which was always a sign something was going to happen. We dropped everything and filed into Bill's smart office, with his secretary outside and real daylight inside. Johnnie was out visiting those 'off on the sick', so there were four of us: Anita, Jim, Tim and me. It was only twenty yards from the piggeries, but it could have been twenty miles for the difference in the quality of the office. Jim glowed in his sweaty blue suit from Burton's, Tim had his clerical grey 'vicar's' suit on, Anita was immaculate in trousers with big flares and tank top over a blouse. I was jacketless, top button of my shirt undone, and tie hanging loose. We chatted, thankfully Johnnie was not there with his roll ups, and then Bill called us to order.

'I think you all know that the company runs a two-month full time training event for prospective superintendents in a local hotel...'

'I smell overtime,' interjected Jim, rubbing his hands.

'There are two candidates from Liverpool, two from Dagenham and one from Wales. Now, one of our eagle-eyed accounts assistants has spotted our trainees have been submitting dinner invoices with consecutive numbers,' continued Bill. Anita cut across,

'The same one that spotted the doctor's notes from the same pad?'

'As it happens, yes.'

'So, two of you need to meet up with a PO from London and one from Wales and get to the Cottons Hotel near

Knutsford tomorrow and conduct investigatory interviews. It's potentially serious. Remember these are some of our highest calibre general foremen and it is one of only two courses this year and the only one run in our area.'

'Jim, you're related to the press shop trainee Superintendent Ratcliffe, so you can't be involved…'

'Bloody hell, he's about five times removed, I only see him for a bevy at funerals,' said Jim. Everyone else laughed, and I said, 'I may be being slow here, but what exactly are they supposed to have done?'

'Probably eating cheap and putting in claims for Steak Diane and Hirondelle,' said Jim slyly.

'Something like that,' said Bill, 'You need to interview them and find out. You'll need to sort out between you which two of the three of you do it.'

On the way back to our offices Tim said, 'What ho chaps, sounds like your forged sick notes case and I'm a bit behind with the plant committee minutes, would it be ok if I ducked on this?'

'It's ok with me if Frank is alright with it too,' said Anita, looking sideways at me.

'It's fine,' I said. I was secretly pleased, I wanted to see if I could find out what Anita's casual remark about her supposed fiancé meant. I knew I'd rationalised it would be easier not to work so closely with Anita again, not after the brush off outside my flat. I was trying not to feel oversensitive, but it would just be easier not to have to see her up close all the bloody time.

'Then let's go upstairs and see what more info the accountant guy has then,' said Anita.

The accountant was vague; he said there weren't even supposed to be receipts at all, as it was an inclusive deal with the hotel for the whole training course. But they were submitting receipts for food from the menu and they were being signed off.

'From the hotel restaurant or outside restaurants?' asked Anita.

'Just the hotel restaurant,' the accountant said.

We tramped back down the stairs, deep in our own thoughts when Bill saw us.

'Hi both. You're meeting the other POs at northbound Knutsford service station on the M6 nine tomorrow, and a teleconference debrief with the other sites at four, ok?' said Bill.

I was going to borrow a company pool car, but Anita offered to pick me up at eight as she would have to pass my flat to get to the M6.

'Umm, seven-thirty would be better, I'd love a Wimpy breakfast,' I said.

'Yes Frank, I think not,' said Anita deadpan.

'They do Danish and filter coffee as well.' We both smiled and agreed the earlier time.

The next morning, I watched out of the window for Anita's car to come round the corner of the flats. Within ten minutes we were driving past the Halewood car factories and in the damp air, the solvent smell of the paint shop wafted through the car.

'I love that smell,' I said absentmindedly.

'The smell of money,' said Anita, half joking, quoting a film she couldn't remember.

Very soon we were approaching the Widnes Bridge where the more unpleasant smells of agrochemicals hung in the air; I held my nose purposely and Anita laughed. By the time we got to Knutsford I realised we couldn't join the service area from the road we were on. We found a 'no entry' service road, and I insisted we go through it much to Anita's concern. I had relaxed, I was amused with Anita over her perturbation with the no entry sign, it was a bit like her attitude to the Red Lion. It still upset me that she was getting into some kind of arranged marriage, but I put that to the back of my mind.

I imitated Tim when we got to the Wimpy,

'What ho, tuck's up,' and joined the queue while Anita went to find the Danish shop. At nine-fifteen we both realised there was no one else there and that we might need to be on the other side of the motorway. We rushed over the bridge to find two men in suits talking, presumably company POs like ourselves.

John, the Welshman, was a bit older than the normal run of the mill PO that I had met; he was more like Jim with his three piece and broken nose. The man from Dagenham, David, was dressed like a head waiter in a black suit.

After introductions, John had said, 'I've just been telling David my card is heavily marked, our trainee is the best on the plant and well favoured by our plant manager.'

David butted in, 'Well, I've had no cards marked, and have an open mind. Our finance people were worried that the Liverpool accountant didn't really have any detail for the alleged offence though.'

'Ok,' I said. 'The brief we've had is that we must interview the five trainees involved in parallel and ask open questions about how they are paying for their dinners. No one is assuming capital offences or anything. I think because they are potential future senior managers, it's being treated very seriously, that's why we're here.' I looked at Anita and she nodded in agreement. We drove to the hotel, a modern affair called The Cottons, about five minutes from the motorway services but literally in the middle of nowhere. We met the course training manager Bob, who was not resident for most of the course. He explained that there shouldn't be a need for receipts to be signed off back at the factories at all, as they had an all-inclusive deal for the event which included full board, conference rooms and so on.

Anita and I started our interview with the press shop general foreman who was the distant relative of Jim, George Ratcliffe, a huge bruiser of a man.

'George, just walk us through how you order and receipt for the evening dinners while you're on this course.'

George said, 'Well, the per diem allowance only allows us to cover the day's set meal, we can't order what we want like, à la carte.' He handed over two set menus from the previous week.

'One day it's braised kidneys, the next day it's liver and onions. We've had enough of eating offal, we really have. If it's not offal, it's something like pork belly. So, I've been eating off the proper menu, submitting expenses and they've been signed off, so I've done nothing wrong in my view.'

I thought for a moment and then said, 'Right, but if the set menu was part of the deal you have no need for receipts at all, surely?'

'Yes, that's why the waitress gave us a pad of receipts so we could claim for what we actually ate. It's all in, so we don't technically need receipts. We're not all doing that, but I'm not grassing anyone up.'

Anita came in with,

'Doing what? Like going into Knutsford to eat?'

'You'll have to find out for yourselves, you're personnel aren't you? All I would say is, the hotel knows the set menu is not really suitable for months on end, they've said that to the company and been ignored.'

'George, you're a trainee senior manager, you're supposed to provide leadership,' I said. George ignored the comment.

'And you're saying the waitress gave you the book of receipts, you didn't steal it?' I continued.

'Ask her, but she gave it to Geoff not me.'

'We will,' said Anita quietly, as he left.

Just before we could begin to discuss the interview, David from London came in.

'My guy says your Wittings is the fiddler. He claims à la carte, but in fact eats the set menus every night which isn't on. He's cheating the system. I suggest you ask him for an explanation.' He then left.

The second senior management trainee came in; he was an older PPC subassembly general foreman, the one David had mentioned. Anita explained the background to why we were interviewing him, and then started with a direct question.

'Are you eating the set menu every night but claiming à la carte on expenses?'

He looked at us weasel-like but said nothing; I could see his mind turning over through his shifting eyes.

'Yes, everyone else is having à la carte, and claiming for it. All I'm doing is forgoing the pleasure and sticking with the set menu and saving myself the money.'

'But they're claiming for what they've eaten, you're not.' said Anita.

'That's true but I could be, couldn't I? So, it's no loss to the company is it?' he said incredulously.

'Sounds like potential fraud to me Geoff,' I said. We went round in circles, until we eventually adjourned for the lunch time wrap up session. Anita and I didn't need to say anything to each other as it was obvious what was happening.

We sat round a table, having invited the training manager Bob to join us.

It became clear in the wrap up that Bob, in negotiating his all-inclusive training package, had no idea that the individuals were submitting receipts and having them authorised back in their plants. He would stop it forthwith he said.

David disagreed,

'There's no way the hotel we use in Ilford, when we run this course would dare serve offal three days a week and on the fourth pork offcut. If they're stuck here for two months, I'll be saying to our finance people they should keep paying expenses. If we must pay more for the course than you Bob have allowed, we will. Ruddy offal, no way.'

John added, 'Well boyos, been a bit of a wasted day for me, and our plant manager will be delighted when I tell him it's an admin cockup after all.'

Anita and I looked at each other, then Anita said she would go and speak to the waitress for a minute to confirm the receipt book story.

While we waited for Anita, I was fascinated to hear that in Wales because of all the recent pit and steel closures, the employment environment was so bad that they didn't have any serious strike culture. Anita reappeared.

'The waitress says she gets a lot of requests to fudge receipts for conference customers. She said there was only one of them, our guy from Liverpool, who demanded a receipt for more than he'd purchased, and she'd diplomatically left a receipt book so he could do it himself.'

David and John stood up together and David said, 'Good luck you two. I will be recommending no action at my end, ok?' and then they nodded and left. We thanked Bob for his time, said we would be in touch tomorrow about George and left him mumbling about the course.

Anita's car was warm and smelt faintly of her perfume; we headed out and back towards the M56 motorway and Liverpool.

She looked sideways at me. 'Before you go to sleep, what are we saying George is likely to be guilty of?'

'Ummm, well he was prepared to eat the admittedly crap food but claim for more and keep the cash for himself. Possibly fiddling expenses, embezzlement, petty fraud or whatever,' I replied dozily.

'Do you think it's gross misconduct?'

'Umm, it could be but if he just got a final warning to teach him a lesson, I would have no problem.'

'Isn't that a double standard?' said Anita.

'The whole thing is a cockup. The factories didn't know the trainees shouldn't have been submitting expenses for any kind of dinner at all, which is Bob the trainer's fault. The other trainees shouldn't have used the receipt book, but they did, which is some kind of minor offence. The food was terrible, and the policy should be changed so I'm not being absolutist, I think you can see it from both sides.'

'Yes, but George was outright fiddling expenses,' said Anita sternly.

'Yes, he was. Whether it's gross misconduct in this situation, I'm less sure of…but it's your area, so one for you and staff personnel,' I said. I sat up as I realised I was being a bit dismissive.

'We certainly wasted the time of the other two, travelling all that way. It was a bit of an embarrassment but maybe they should have done telephone interviews or something,' I said.

As we hummed along and turned over the Runcorn-Widnes Bridge, my eyes turned to the left.

'Do you want to stop for lunch at the Childe?' I said.

Anita raised her eyebrows,

'Thanks, but no thanks, we need to get back.'

'Yeah, you're right. Pie and chips in the canteen again then.'

'You can actually get a cheese omelette or salad you know,' said Anita.

I didn't respond, just enjoyed sitting back being driven. I was doing my best not to see Anita as someone I yearned for any more, but my eyes were drawn to her legs occasionally.

'Why don't we go after work tonight, instead?'

I sat up blinking, wondering if I'd heard that right.

'After work?'

'Yes.'

I looked ahead, trying to get my sleepy brain in gear. I thought for a moment, I could get along just in work time, but an evening would be so difficult. Did she even understand what she was saying, maybe it was a strange Asian cultural thing?

'I'll take that as a "no", shall I?' Anita said casually.

'I'd love to, but I just can't,' I said. She was still looking ahead driving, but turned towards me and said,

'Why not?'

I stared at her incredulous.

'Why not? Why not? Because I'd want to kiss you like we kissed before,' I said in a tight voice.

'And if I said "Yes" to that?' she said quietly, still staring ahead.

'For God's sake,' I said. 'Pull over, pull over in that bus layby,' pointing to one on the left.

Anita ground slowly to a halt. It took me a few seconds to collect myself.

'I... I... what's happened with your pharmacist?'

'It's what my family always wanted, I realised over the weekend it's not what I want.'

'What, so you're not engaged anymore then?' Looking towards her, as she sat with her arms slumped on the wheel.

'There was an understanding' she said hurriedly, 'I never was engaged as such.'

I considered the implications of what she'd just said.

'Bloody hell, Anita,' I said, 'you're one surprising girl!'

She looked at me quizzically and moved slowly back into the traffic.

After a few seconds, I said,

'So, a five o'clock kiss tonight outside the Childe?'

She looked sideways at me for a moment, and smiling broadly she said,

'I really liked the last one, I thought you might have noticed.'

We were both due at the four o'clock teleconference meeting with Eric and Bill, to discuss the training course expenses issue. Eric had his pipe in as normal, not alight at that moment and he was already on the speaker phone with the London and Wales industrial relations managers.

'They must be stuck in bloody traffic, David rang to say the M6 was still blocked after an accident. I suggest we postpone till five anyway.'

My heart sank, I could see drinks with Anita sinking into the abyss of waiting at work for people to ring from hundreds of miles away. Anita saved the day. 'Hi, it's Anita from Halewood here, I think we can save you a bit of time actually.'

'How's that then?' said one of the IRMs, I wasn't sure which.

'All of the POs concluded in our wrap up that John and David had probably wasted their time today. All their trainees were doing was eating à la carte when they were sick of the offal on the set menu and submitting their receipts for the right amounts.'

I got in on the call to support her.

'Hi, Frank Thomas here, yes it was braised kidneys, pigs' liver and belly pork. Technically they shouldn't have been putting in receipts because it was all inclusive, but no one in the factories knew that and the receipts were being signed off.'

Eric came in,

'So, there are no issues with these consecutive receipts that finance spotted at all then?'

Anita came back, 'Unfortunately, one of the Liverpool trainees has done something more serious, which we can discuss locally, I was just saying I don't think London and Wales will need any further involvement at all. That would be David and John's view anyway.'

'That's a bloody relief,' said Dai, the IRM from Wales. 'We don't exactly have many high calibre trainee supers, so we could ill afford to lose one. Right. Ok. Thanks for your time, you lot, and I'll see you next week in London, Eric. Bye everybody.'

Bill looked sternly at Anita and me.

'So, who is it what has he done and has he been suspended?'

I nodded to Anita to speak, Gittings was in her area.

'Well, it was Geoff Gittings in PPC. He certainly deliberately submitted expenses for à la carte food when he was eating the set menu. The others ate the food they were submitting expenses for – that's the difference. The waitress gave Gittings the receipt pad as she knew she couldn't put à la carte through for him as he wasn't eating it, just claiming he had. As he is senior-ish and white collar, of course we did nothing other than investigate.'

Eric spoke, pipe in mouth, looking over the top of his reading glasses.

'Thanks, you two for going. Bill, you had better handle this from here and liaise with John in staff personnel as well. For a trainee senior manager, he has seriously blotted his copybook. The others should get a ticking off about the à la carte, ok.'

I added as we got up to leave, 'I'm not sure the set menu is really acceptable by the way, they don't serve anything like that on the Ilford hotel course according to David the PO there and it seems unfair to impose it up here.'

'Bill, you can look at that with the training people at Head Office, I like a bit of tripe but there should be a choice.' Everyone laughed at the word 'tripe' and we split up and left.

At five o'clock I was on tenterhooks and went to brush my teeth; Jim was using the urinal. He looked sideways at me.

'Well, it's too late for the dentist, so whaddye cleaning your teeth for, Frank?'

'Coffee breath,' I garbled.

'Why don't I believe you?' and he smirked and nudged me as he went back out. I nearly called out for him to wash his bloody hands but decided not to.

I packed up and decamped next door with my coat on, to wait for Anita, who was out on plant somewhere. I hoped she wasn't having second thoughts, but she'd definitely said the engagement was off, hadn't she?'

She walked in, stony faced. I stood up, disconcerted.

'Are you ok?'

'Yes, I'll tell you about it in the pub.' I was relieved she'd not changed her mind.

We walked out together, Anita still obviously thinking about whatever incident she'd just come from.

'Are you still ok with this, Anita?

'No, yes, I mean, I'll be fine in a minute.'

We smiled at each other and separated to go to our cars, which were on different car parks miles away in the damp fluorescent gloom.

I was first at the pub and had decided en route I would not give her the kiss I'd threatened, she was fazed by something.

I leant back on my old Beetle car and admired the funny obelisk outside the pub. I couldn't hide the warm feelings I'd had since Anita had dumbfounded me earlier that day. She drove in, in her smart Escort and looking over at her cheered me further. I walked slowly over to see her, she got out the other side and smoothed down the creases in her trousers. She turned towards me, expectantly.

'Well, I'm waiting.'

I blushed and was about to say I was only joking but couldn't stop myself giving her a long lingering kiss on the lips. She smiled and grabbed my arm and we walked towards the doors, both laughing together at the absurdity of it all.

18

Fight

One morning in December I found myself reluctantly accompanying Jim O'Neill back to the press shop.

'Look, I know it's my patch, but youse did the original interviews with the fighters in me absence so youse have to be there,' whined Jim as we strolled up through the plant. The press shop manager, John May, had a large office up the usual galvanised iron steps to a mezzanine floor. The noise was suppressed in the office but not the vibration. The 1,000-tonne body side presses were ever present, but at least the burning smell of the cutting oils was left downstairs. I looked out at the men stamping metal then passing it down the line to the next set of presses.

John May was an ex-apprentice with an HNC who'd transferred from the Dagenham press shop, about forty-five, silver haired and well groomed. Vinny something or other was there, a shop steward I'd seen in Jim's office a few times; he looked like a rat that had emerged from a tunnel.

'Right, let's get on then, said John. We have the two alleged fighters, the foreman and three witnesses to see this morning. Let's start with the two fighters.' Jim went out to get them. Ron an Irish man, who was also originally from Dagenham, had a bandaged hand and a plaster on his face. When I'd seen him the day before, he'd been covered in blood. Jim surprised me by also bringing in the other guy at the same time, Tom, who had a badly bruised eye and face.

The foreman was called as a first witness. He was paunchy, middle aged with a green work coat on.

'Err, I was tipped off there was an incident in the basement, so I went down to investigate, like. There was about a group of ten men standing in a semicircle and I could hear yelling. Someone shouted I was there, and they dispersed, leaving these two men on their knees.'

Jim asked, 'Did you actually see anyone land a punch or grappling with each other?'

'No. They looked like they'd been fighting so I rang my boss and personnel to come over. The first aider attended to them then Mr Thomas came in and we interviewed them in my office.'

John May then said, 'Ok take a seat, please. Frank, what were their answers to your questions about them fighting?' I looked at my notepad,

'Ron said that he'd slipped and smashed his face on a Vickers guard, and Tom said he walked into a locker room door.' I said. 'Looking at the state of them I didn't believe them, and I said they were suspended forthwith for fighting on company premises and to come back today.'

Both of them sat there and said there was definitely no fight, just a heated argument about the football derby result and both swore on their children's lives that no one threw any punches. I was gobsmacked by the audacity of their lies.

Vinny the steward was asked to comment. 'Look there are no witnesses to any fight, there aren't even any complaints from these two about the other so there was no fight. Even your own foreman says he didn't see a fight. There's no case to answer.'

There was a long silence till John called an adjournment leaving himself, Jim and me in the room. Jim looked from face to face, embarrassed.

'Ok, we all know the traditional way of the press shop sorting out differences has been the basement, but we've largely stamped it out. We don't want to see it happening anymore.' Then holding open the palms of his hands he raised his eyebrows and said, 'With no witnesses here, there's nothing we can do.'

I was annoyed, I wasn't completely sure if management had been duped by the witnesses or whether they were just complicit in a cover up; I strongly suspected the latter.

'I saw the state of them last night, there was blood everywhere, and it's a complete fabrication that one walked into a locker and the other a guard. Are you seriously expecting me to believe that?'

'We're not daft, man,' retorted John, clearly annoyed. 'If no one makes a complaint and the foreman doesn't see a punch being landed, if we go ahead and dismiss them, we will just lose on appeal, isn't that right Jim?'

'I'm afraid so,' said Jim, looking embarrassed.

'I thought this was 1978 not 1878,' I said. 'Are we now turning a blind eye to staff sorting out differences with their fists in the factory?'

'Welcome to the press shop mate,' said Jim before he could stop himself. I sat there seething with indignation. I would definitely take it up with Bill when I got back to the office.

Jim went out to see the steward in private,

'Vinny says they'll accept verbal warnings with no appeal for "conduct unbecoming" and causing management all this hassle,' he said sheepishly. John called the two men back in with the steward and announced the verdict, and they left.

'What's "conduct unbecoming" then, a new word for a press shop cover up?' I said. Jim shepherded me out of the door before John lost his temper.

On the way back still annoyed, I said, 'Have you discussed this with Bill?'

'Of course not, Bill's last job was the press shop PO; he knows how things are here. I look on the bright side, like verbal warnings means no paperwork for me.'

What a nightmare bloody place this is, I said to myself.

19

Ripper

One Monday, Bill summoned us all to a meeting at nine. We got coffee, said our hellos and trooped off to Bill's office. I was last up the corridor, hoping to speak to Anita but Tim was chatting to her. Anita was as smart and fresh as usual, Jim was muttering about overtime opportunities, Tim had his notebook and pen like a cub reporter and Johnnie had his *Racing Post*. What a collection, I thought. I looked down at myself in my Burton's grey suit with mismatched blue woollen tie.

Bill had his sleeves rolled up with strange metal sleeve holder-uppers.

'Morning all. A number of new things are going down which means reprioritising whatever you are doing,' scanning our faces.

'First of all, Jim, I want you to liaise with the police (we all looked at each other) as they want to interview three operators about the Ripper murders.'

'They think the Yorkshire Ripper is here?' asked Jim excitedly.

'They say they're not necessarily arresting anyone, but there are three operators they want to question about their movements on certain days around the Leeds red light district. If you could use your office as the interview base, they don't want the union stewards involved.'

Tim cut in. 'What happens if they demand their steward is present?'

'They'll threaten to arrest them and take them to the main Bridewell,' said Bill.

'Bridewell?' asked Tim inquisitively.

'The big piggery in the centre of town,' said Jim rolling his eyes.

'Piggery?'

'Cop shop, police station!' shouted Jim.

'There's more,' said Bill. Public relations do not want headlines like "Company workers interviewed in Ripper murders" so try and keep a lid on it. They also asked me if we had anyone we knew with a distinct north east accent, but I couldn't think of anyone frankly.'

Jim said, 'I can't either, though there's someone from Newcastle in the press shop, is that the same place? I thought they were all tarts in Leeds that he'd murdered though.'

Anita sniffed, 'the last one was a building society clerk in Halifax; I don't think you can hold that job down and be a street tart on the side Jim.'

'So why are they interested in Leeds red light visitors from here then?' retorted Jim.

'Ok, that's enough you two. Frank, I know it's Jim's area but there's a catering assistant who's submitted a false application for a mortgage. Doris in personnel records will brief you; if it's not a simple dismissal let me know.'

'Anita and Johnnie, another one in Jim's area. Sadly, an ex-shop steward is having his stomach pumped from whiskey poisoning after the nightshift. Check out if he drank it here to be that bad this morning.'

'Probably Dusty Miller then,' said Jim. Bill looked at him intently.

'Johnnie, if you get down the hospital now. Anita, can you try and find out what his foreman knew, including the last time he spoke to him last night, are his mates covering for him, etc. Oh, can you brief me on the latest on the cottaging case as well?'

'Well, if it's the press shop, from my recent experience I would say "Yes" a cover up…' I said looking directly at Jim. He stared at his greasy brown suede shoes.

Tim said,

'What about me?'

'You'll have to handle any dispute, disciplinary or whatever across the whole plant that can't be put off, ok?'

'Right-oh,' said Tim.

'You can take your coffees with you,' dismissing us all. We walked back, I found myself next to Jim.

'Today's paper does say the Ripper has been sending in cassette tapes with a Wearside accent.'

Anita and Johnnie went into his office together, so I gave up on trying to ask how the weekend had gone. I read the file from personnel records that Bill's secretary had given me and rearranged what had been planned for the day. Half an hour later I heard Anita go into her office, but she was on the phone, so I went in as soon as she was off it.

Before I could speak, a glum Anita said, 'That was Johnnie from the hospital. The guy has just died from acute alcohol poisoning.'

'Oh, I'm sorry to hear that. What do you do now then, do you continue the investigation in the press shop?'

'I don't know, I suppose there will be an inquest... I'll go and see Bill for some advice,' and she got up to go.

'Well, if you fancy a chat after work, I'm free,' I said hopefully.

'Let's see where we are at five o'clock then,' replied Anita neutrally.

I trudged up to personnel records where thousands of Roneo files were kept, including a personal file on every employee. I managed to corner the bustling Doris, the supervisor. She was about fifty, slim and efficiently managing the four clerks it took to keep the records straight. I had always thought her an officious bureaucrat from previous dealings as everything with her was always black and white.

'Hello there. Bill didn't give me much detail, what is it this catering assistant has supposedly done?' Doris was immediately on the defensive, noting my sceptical tone.

'Well, the list is long. She lied about her wages, where she said she gets £75 a week when it's only £65. She also lied about her overtime earnings too. We always see it as attempted fraud and dismiss, as it damages our reputation with the banks and building societies.'

'Seriously? Seems a bit harsh to me, she's not exactly the works accountant, is she?' I said.

'No, but she handles the money in the cash till in the canteen though,' said Doris sternly.

'Yeah, but she's not shoplifting, is she?'

I left, gruffly muttering. I knew college mates in London who were regularly being inventive to get mortgages for a property; there were even 'brokers' who did it professionally down there. I went back to my office, rang the canteen manageress who saw it all as a personnel matter, nothing to do with her. She said the accused was a bit 'flighty' but a good worker and got on well with the customers. I thought that if there was a steward I trusted in the area I would want him in the meeting with her, but as I didn't know any in the canteen, I would ask to see her on her own. I was investigating not disciplining so I could take any future criticism on the chin for there not being a steward present. At least that way, she might tell me the truth. I knew it was Jim's area and if he was investigating, he wouldn't care a jot either way, so why was I going to all this trouble? She could be a complete scally, but I knew from experience that I would want to hear her side of the story, not just what Doris alleged it was.

Her name was Stella, she was about thirty but looked younger with a punk-like hairstyle and a striking gaunt face. She must have been nearly six feet tall. She was nervous on being called to personnel, she had orangey eyes darting around like a Russian cat. I sat her down and got her a coffee.

'Stella, I'm Frank Thomas. I know Jim's your PO, but he's tied up…'

'Oh yeah, the police are in interviewing for the Ripper,' she said breathlessly.

'Wow,' I said laughing, 'the jungle drums are quick here.'

'That's the canteen for you, we hear a lot.'

'Ok. Now there's the matter of your mortgage application…' she cut across me, eyes burning fiercely.

'I've been refused, I had a letter from the Cheshire Building Society last week, saying I don't earn enough.'

I realised her supervisor had not even told her what the interview was for and sighed, 'Right well, the thing is Stella, exaggerating your wages on the mortgage application form is seen as a serious thing by the company.'

'I know but I could have coped, I've given up smoking, hardly drink and could eat less to ensure we paid it,' she said defiantly.

'We?' I said puzzled as I thought the application was in her name only.

'Me and my son Paul. I've got to get him away from the gobshites in Speke to a house with a decent school where he won't be bullied. He's a bit of a slow learner, he's in the bottom class and they call him "Soft Paul". There's a really good special school in Widnes which will take him, but we've got to live near there first to get him in.'

'Ok,' I said, more to myself than her. I really hated these types of cases, I always rationally understood the company personnel position but there was never any flexibility. Everybody in personnel was always concerned about avoiding establishing a custom and practice that could be used in future cases. Doing what was fair or right never came into it which pissed me off.

There were tears forming in her eyes, I glanced to where my box of tissues were.

'Are you saying I might be on the stones? I'm just trying to better myself, that's all. If I lose this job we're finished, he's finished…' she started to well up and I passed the tissues and looked away, trying to give her some dignity.

I knew I had been changed by my time in the company; I still had no time for militants pulling the company down but it looked like she was just trying to give her son a chance in a better school. She eventually stopped sobbing, and her eyes shone.

I picked up the file and made up my mind. Sod it. One thing I'd learnt in my short time at work is that you can occasionally subvert bureaucracy from within. She wasn't that far away from the figure she needed for the mortgage; if she did give up smoking and drinking, she could probably do it – the company should give her a chance not bloody dismiss her...

'Stella, looking at your payslips, you've misunderstood gross and net pay, haven't you?'

'Have I? She looked startled.

'Yes, you've put down the wrong one, and I'm accepting it as a genuine mistake on your part. On the overtime, you've put down the wrong figure as well.'

'Have I?'

I looked up, wondering what I was doing.

'Now, I'll be writing the notes for this investigation, and if anyone else questions you on this, this is what you'll need to say.'

She sat upright, beginning to look relieved.

'I asked if you wanted a shop steward and you said no, I'm writing that down, right?'

'Yes'

'Good, well the meeting's over, there will be no further action. Just tell the manageress it was a clarification meeting only, she can ring me if she needs to.'

I closed the file with a flourish. I peered over the folder into her eyes, they certainly were unusual.

'Listen, don't give up. Looking at this, you're not far away from the amount you need. If I can arrange for you to do a couple of months' worth of weekend overtime for the twelve-hour shift lads that'll probably do it. If I organise that, will you be able to do it with your child responsibilities?' She nodded.

'It will definitely fix your case. Then just reapply and pop in and see me on the way to your shift. I'll help you check the wages figures.'

'I, I, don't know what to say, yes, yes. Are they all as nice as you in labour relations?'

I stood up, laughing, 'No,' and opened the door for her. As I ushered her out, she caught me by surprise by reaching up and kissing me on the cheek. I blushed and instantly looked round to see if anyone was watching.

'Double sausage for you at dinner time,' she added smiling.

'Honestly, Stella, I don't want anything, I'm just doing my job.'

'Everybody wants something, Mr Thomas,' and then she was gone.

I sat down, a bit flustered. I touched my cheek where she'd kissed it and drank my coffee thoughtfully. I knew I hadn't heard the last of this, Bill would hear the result through Doris in Records and Jim would be suspicious. But as I hadn't involved the union or local management, I couldn't really see how any custom and practice was being set or anyone could overrule me. Job done.

I thought about her parting remark, what did I want? Was it the ego of power or was I just up for helping one person in a factory of robotic policies and occasionally stupid procedures?

I closed my eyes and drifted half off. Bill opened the door,

'Five o'clock debrief, if you can stay awake.'

I could see they all looked a lot more tired than at the morning meeting. Jim started, everyone looking intently at him because of the Ripper interviews.

'The Rozzers interviewed them for five hours,' noticing Tim's quizzical expression and added 'police I mean.' Two were of no interest but Fred Tambling from Framing was. Turns out, he's from Leeds and he goes back on weekends apparently kerb crawling in Chapeltown.' There was a stunned silence from everyone.

'So, they've logged his number plates several times, that's why they're here. Anyway, he admitted that but they didn't arrest him, so they presumably don't think he's the Ripper. I was kicked out after the introductions, so I don't know the details.'

'Will he be charged with soliciting?' said Tim.

'The rozzers think not, they said they would show his picture to some of the tarts there but unless they finger him for violence or something, he's off scot free. They did search his locker though, but there were no claw hammers...'

'Ok Jim, no black humour on this, thanks. I guess the scare is over on that then. Such a horrible case, I hope they catch the bugger soon,' said Bill. Everyone else started talking about the Ripper murders; they had been headline news every week for what seemed like years. Bill stroked his moustache and looked around.

'Ok. Right. Anita, Johnnie, what's the latest on Miller, I saw it was in the *Echo*.'

Anita looked at her notes.

'Our doc says he was probably drunk before work and topped it up while here. Two half empty bottles of whiskey were found near where he works, but we can't be sure if it they were actually drunk last night.'

Jim butted in,

'Have the lads been covering for him, then?

'Well, the foreman saw him at a distance doing subassembly work at break time. Whether he skipped off after that he didn't know. As it's "job and finish" it's not clear. Whether the others just covered up for him by doing his work, no one is saying,' she shrugged.

Jim added, 'It was well known he was an alky like, but he was well liked.'

Bill thought for a moment, then said, 'Next steps on the case?'

Anita answered, 'We are putting it on hold until the inquest is complete, the site doctor will keep in touch with the coroner and we'll make a statement then. Given his death today, there's no need for any disciplinary inquiry obviously.'

The room was quiet.

'Ok, thanks, keep me informed. What an incredibly sad case. I guess Jim, you can handle the future discussions now the Ripper case seems sorted.'

'Frank?' said Bill, looking to me. I sounded as casual as I could.

'Nothing, I'm afraid. A case of someone misunderstanding her pay slip, certainly not fraud. I've investigated it thoroughly and sent her back to work.'

Bill frowned and looked at me. Jim raised his eyebrows but said nothing.

We broke up and walked back to the piggeries, Jim followed me into the office.

'Err, isn't Stella that lanky fit-looking bird behind the counter in the canteen?'

'And?' I said, self-conscious but hoping it didn't show.

Jim touched his nose,

'If there's somethin' fishy goin' down here I'll find out,' and slowly backed out, eyes on me.

I shrugged it off and went into Anita's office; she looked bothered for once and was staring at the filing cabinet.

'Are you ok?'

'Phew yes, his workmates didn't know he'd died so it was pretty upsetting telling them in the plant tearoom. I thought Johnnie was good, credit to him for the way he handled things.' She paused seeming distracted,

'I've never had to do something like that before, tell someone's workmate a colleague has died. They were fond of him, that's why they covered for him when he was incapable, but that may have hastened his death. I think some of them now realise that, so it was all very emotional.'

'Thankfully, that's one personnel experience I've never had,' I said.

'Would you mind if we didn't meet after work tonight, I think I need to get home, have a bath and just sleep.'

'Sure. I'll see you tomorrow,' I said.

20

Demarcation

Anita was in early. It must be a work commitment as she was an evening person from what I could tell. I signalled did she want a coffee and she said yes, but almost straight away, Bill walked in.

'Morning both, hope you are well, because Jim's off sick with gout.'

'Must be too much caviar or black pudding,' I said.

'I've heard it's very painful,' said Anita with a serious face.

'Yeah, whatever, I get the sympathy,' said Bill smiling. 'I still need to reallocate some of his work that can't wait though. Frank, there are some battery thefts you can deal with.'

'Battery thefts? Surely they're in the PTA plant?'

'Yes but, two stacker truck drivers from here were caught by security taking them out.'

'Ok,' I said.

'Anita, there's a die setter dispute kicking off in the press shop too.'

'Die, what's that, what does it mean?' she replied.

'The shape cut by the press itself,' I said, kicking myself for coming over as a know it all.

'Where's Tim this morning? said Bill.

'Butler not got him up yet,' I said.

'No choice then Anita, here's the paperwork,' said Bill.

'Why don't we swop Bill, I know the press shop a bit better?'

'No. You need to be free this afternoon for the drillings dispute meeting in your area, so it will have to be Anita.' Bill frowned and left. Trying to be helpful but conscious of being patronising, I said to Anita who had opened the file, 'What's the issue then?'

'Looks like die setters are refusing to train setter operators and are threatening industrial action about it,' and rolled her eyes.

'Yeah, sounds like some kind of demarcation issue…' Anita cut across me sharply, 'How do you know that?'

'I don't, just surmising that's all. Is everything all right?' I enquired.

'No, it's not. How many women are there in the press shop?

'Umm, none, not even in the office there,' I said sensing what was coming next.

'It's not a great start to the day going up there; every other person I walk by stares at me like I'm a walking pair of tits. The others just whistle or do monkey gestures.'

I blushed.

'There's no women in the body plant production lines either and I get monkey gestures when I walk through as well.'

'This is 1979, women can work shifts, why aren't there any?' she was working herself up into an indignant anger.

'You've done recruitment, they never apply for the jobs, do they?' I said. 'And how many men are there in the seat trimming area in PTA? None!'

'There's not even a female toilet in the press shop, I bet you didn't know that?'

'True, I didn't know. Well, our priority is to make 836 cars a day, we can sort out the gender stereotypes when we all have jobs to come to first.'

Anita looked pointedly down at her folder, I felt myself being dismissed and stepped out back into the corridor and into my office, annoyed by the way our conversation had gone out of control in an instant.

I opened the file on my desk and was intrigued but puzzled. Two forklift drivers had been found with a battery each in the last month, and more when the police searched their houses.

Both had been dismissed that week; Jim's letters were on the file, there had been no appeals so what exactly was I to do today? I went in to see if Bill was in his office. He was and his reply to the question was in French.

'An "encourage d'autres" note for the noticeboards, that's it,' said Bill. Ten minutes later I had written: 'Two employees have been found guilty of the theft of batteries and sentenced to three months imprisonment and have subsequently been dismissed from the service of the company.'

It was slightly archaic but would do. I gave it to June, Bill's secretary, who would type it on letterhead and Roneo it for all the company notice boards. Job done.

I knew I couldn't really get what it was like to be a woman in an all-male working environment; the porn and nudes in the tea rooms I could see but there were no whistles or cat calls whenever I was on the shop floor with Anita. I could empathise that it must be wearing, as the job could be unpleasant any day of the week without cat calls making it worse. I breezed into her office, said I was free and as the press shop was new to both of us, could I go with her? (I had always had a sneaking admiration for her wanting to do whatever this job entailed.) She said, 'Ok smartass, that's fine.'

We climbed the press shop office gangway stairs to find the press shop manager John May already there. He looked up, surprised.

'We don't need you, love,' he said out of the side of his mouth.

'Oh yes, and why's that then?' Anita said firmly.

'I've discussed a new proposal with the steward, and we're close to agreement. I'll write it up and send it to Jim to issue and file.'

'Jim's off sick, could be gone a long time,' Anita replied.

'It'll wait.'

I thought May was patronising with his tone but thought he probably would've been with me as well. It may have been because she was a woman, but it could also be because he'd done a dodgy deal with Jim that he didn't want anyone else knowing about. Well, it wasn't our area, and if that's the way they wanted it, it was fine by me as we both had enough to do already.

'Why didn't you tell Bill twenty minutes ago and save us the walk?' I said.

'Because we've only just this minute sorted it, I was going to ring him now.'

Lying bastard, I thought, but Anita smiled turned round and left. I knew now why she hated the press shop, the macho managers, the vibration, smell, the whole place.

I was surprised that evening, on how the EEC discussions had played out on Britain's budget rebate. Thatcher was certainly putting her foot down and demanding a huge refund, and I was impressed with her assertiveness. 'I want my money back,' she was reported as having said. I cooked myself a healthy dinner of faggots, oven chips and processed peas. Not having brought home any paperwork, I decided to walk to my local pub for a pint.

In the Black Bull pub, I picked up a *Liverpool Echo* that someone must have left behind. It was surprisingly empty; it was definitely a decent pub with no jukebox or pinball machine noises. The paper was full of local car industry woes. Pressed Steel Fisher car bodies in Liverpool had 500 paint shop staff on strike due to a job grading issue. Vauxhall's in Ellesmere Port over the water had 7000 staff on the fifth week of a pay strike. The article was amusing for me, as management were reported as having found £75,000 worth of stolen car parts in employee rest areas which were 'no-go' when the plant was working. I made a mental note to check out if employee rest areas were 'no-go' in my plant when I got into work. On my second pint, I noticed Fiat was investing further in Poland and Yugoslavia as well as Brazil. To cap it all, 32,000 Rolls Royce aviation staff were 'locked out on a pay strike' with the new Tory Industry

Secretary refusing to meet either unions or the management for 'beer and sandwiches.' Maybe things were really changing, I said to myself as I got up to walk home.

The months blurred into each other for me that summer of 1979; I thought that my colleagues and I were realistically working at almost 100%. Every day there was a mountain of work to get through, most of it unplanned and always urgent. I'd hardly seen Anita at work, she'd never rearranged the pub visit we had planned so I'd never found out what had happened at the Leicester weekend. We had gradually become a little distant, but although I'd wracked my brains I couldn't get why and had too much pride to ask. After a month of worrying about how to speak to Anita, I realised I had taken my usual default way out and just thrown myself into work.

I still had the long running drillings dispute which at times depressed me. Normally, I knew the day to day 'human' issues and the variety of ridiculous things that happened kept me challenged and amused. This dispute though had been like a running sore for nine months and we must have lost hundreds of cars over the many shifts.

One Thursday, Willie John and Lenny Lobo strolled into my office unannounced.

'To what do I owe this dubious pleasure gents?' I said.

'Right dere,' said Lenny.

'Frank son, you've now got five mini disputes in bits of framing and drillings and your management are no listening,' said Willie.

'When you're losing twenty-five cars every shift, what do you expect?' I said...

'With such shite management, whaddye expect?' replied Willie.

'A shite workforce attitude more like,' I replied...

'Ok, let's stop slaggin' each other off, right?' said Lenny.

'I told you Lenny, he's got a fuckin' screw loose,' said Willie looking at me.

'Me? The softest PO on site mate, and you know it,' I said.

'Most likely to ignore every personnel procedure more like,' laughed Willie. He continued, 'Look, the option drillings on vinyl roofs are up, the van mix is causing havoc in the rough discing booths, the LCD springs and hinges workload is all over the show.'

'Bollocks,' I said. 'The industrial engineers aren't wrong; your lads just want more time for themselves.'

Lenny came in,

'The manning's too tight like, we all know…'

'Bollocks. The more cars lost, the more overtime there is, but no one sees the extra costs are killing us all. You read the papers, do you see where all the investment is going – we're the next British Leyland.'

'Oh yeah, the big boss is in today's paper, we made £100 million despite the nine-week strike last year, so he can fuckin' spend some on manning…' Lenny was watching from face to face like a ping pong match as our voices got louder and louder.

'Bollocks. It's the Germans, the Spanish and the Brazilians who are taking our jobs, that's the problem…'

'And he got an 80% pay rise, you'll hear more of that when we present this year's pay claim,' said Willie in a flourish.

We rested for a moment. Willie put on his soft conciliatory Scottish brogue, 'In the other plant areas your mates in personnel, they act more of an intermediary you know, lean on line management. You don't, you're harder line than the bleedin' line management…'

'Bollocks,' I shouted (I noticed Anita and Tim peering through the glass into my office).

Lenny tried to calm us down.

'Frank son, it's like this. If I don't come back with some concessions from management, I'm goin' to be opposed at the steward election. The other areas in body plant are givin' the lads some, all except your area. It's really hurtin' me, la. I'm tellin' yuh.'

'Bollocks,' I said again, before I could stop myself.

'Lenny, we've said our piece. Yon ball is in his hands. I fear for you Lenny, it's like talkin' to soft Mick not a PO when yuh talkin' to him.'

'Bollocks.' They left, shaking their heads.

I looked around the office, with my head in my hands, staring at the half glass metal door. Of course, they were half right. If the other POs were encouraging compromises my sticking out for management to work to engineering study standards put me in a difficult position. Bastards. Anita appeared unannounced, her navy pencil skirt and check top catching my eye. I shrugged.

'What was all the swearing about?' she asked.

'Oh, just Willie and Lenny having a go about me being hard line on manning standards,' I said wearily.

She said, 'I think I might agree with them on that.'

'Seriously?' I said perturbed.

'For someone interested in politics you don't do political nous, do you?' said Anita.

I was worn out, deflated. I began to think why did I bother, why not roll over like everyone else?

'Well, I guess I don't have the wisdom of a Business MBA, do I?' I said.

Anita looked at me, got up and left the office without speaking.

'Sorry, that was a cheap remark...' but she was walking out.

Bill appeared and beckoned Anita back into my office.

'What was a cheap remark?' he said.

'Oh, it's a long story never mind,' I said.

'Well, I've got some bad news for you both.' Anita sat down.

'You both need to appear at the Industrial Tribunal on the steward pub glasses case.'

'For God's sake... sorry?' I said.

'But I thought he admitted being there?' said Anita puzzled.

'He does, but he's disputing the time in the pub so the photos with the time printed on are the best evidence apparently,' said Bill. I immediately thought of the pictures of Anita's legs; whatever happened to them, she'd never said. I was already looking forward to going as I'd only ever observed at a tribunal before and it would be good experience for me to take part in one. I suspected Anita was not.

'Worse. The barrister representing us wants to see you in Head Office the day after tomorrow, so cancel whatever and get a pool car or train to London.'

'Isn't that a bit over the top? What can we be questioned on? We were just there and took photos at whatever time.' Said Anita.

'PTA says the union lawyer will want to cross-examine you both, I'll drop addresses etc on one of your desks, sorry,' and left.

Anita looked down and sighed heavily.

'Are you ok? Do you want some water?' I said.

'Thanks, yes', and I quickly fetched a white plastic cup from the little fountain we had. I just didn't get it, she was clever articulate so how could she be fazed by this?

'Why are you so worried about the tribunal, I've never been a witness in one either.'

'I'm not, more having to relive the Red Lion incident again.'

I thought for a moment. I just didn't understand what was upsetting about it. Yes it was unpleasant but in the grander scheme of things…

'Ok. Look, do you want to meet at the Childe after work and discuss tomorrow? I'll need to get the paperwork first, I'm sure I've forgotten more than I remember.'

'Yes, thanks that would be good. Can we make it that pub in Gateacre near you, the Black Bull or whatever it's called instead, as it's on the way home for me?'

'Sure' I said.

'I'll tidy my desk and go now, I'm not up to doing anything else,' and then she smiled wanly and left my office. She wafted past leaving some very faint perfume smell. I realised I could only recognise my Brut 33 spray-on deodorant, the stuff Barry Sheene and Henry Cooper wore.

I was delayed getting to the pub, as I had to dig out the paperwork. Anita was on her own in the lounge; it was old-fashioned with dark hunting scenes and stuffed foxes in glass cases everywhere. It looked like she'd drunk three Babychams, a record I thought. She wanted another and I got a pint of bitter.

'Bloody hell Anita, you're looking a bit forlorn tonight.'

I sat down on the leather bench next to her, patted her hand on the table in a way I hoped was reassuring. She turned her face towards me, her eyes were puffy like she'd been crying.

'I should have had lunch, I feel drunk I do.' She took another large swig of Babycham.

'Do you want some pork scratchings, to keep you going?' I suggested.

'Yuk, no I like crisps, crisps.' She was sounding half cut, so I got two packets of crisps.

'I'm leaving, I'm leaving,' she mumbled and wiped her eyes on a funny yellow silk looking handkerchief. I wasn't sure what she meant and opened a packet for her and handed it over as she'd not actually moved.

'I'm leaving for a job at Head Office,' her voice breaking up.

'Shit,' I said, I'd thought she'd meant leaving the pub. I blew out some air. 'Oh,' I went into my congratulations routine mindlessly while feeling rubbish about it, instantly regretting not having tried harder earlier in the year.

'I haven't accepted yet, it makes me feel like I've been a failure here,' her eyes closed for a second and then she burped.

'Excuse me.'

I knew she was ambitious, I knew she didn't really like the factory environment, who could blame her? I didn't want to think about it right now, it needed time to sink in.

'I've never seen anyone get tipsy in such a short period of time before,' I said.

'You're nice Frank, but I know you care more about bloody cars than people,' she mumbled.

'Deus ex machina ,' I said…

'What?' said Anita, looking at me glass eyed. 'I'd like another one…'

'No way, you've had four …I steadied her as she stood up and leaned against the dark table, trying to get her car keys out.

'Got to get home, don't want to make an… bloody brother Paki bashers…' I pulled her back down and linked my arm in hers and stopped her moving, her head lolled onto my side… what was she on about? No way could she drive; I started fast forwarding the options. I could order her a taxi, but I didn't trust her on her own in this state. I could walk her back to my place, but I didn't want her seeing it even if drunk as she would be sober in the morning.

'Come on girl I'll drive you home,' and started to lift her up.

'I'm not a cat, sounds like I'm a cat,' she mumbled. I half walked her across the room and said to the barmaid,

'Is it ok to leave her car in the car park till tomorrow?'

'Your risk, love' was the deadpan reply.

I never locked my car as no one would steal it, so I just tipped her into the passenger seat and did the belt up, she was still mumbling about a brother, her mum, the tribunal and her new job. I eventually got to her flat and struggled getting her up the three big steps to the Victorian house that had been converted. I'd picked her up once there but had never been inside till now.

The corridor was freshly painted white and led onto a Habitat-type lounge, so I folded her into a weird looking curvy chair.

'Am hungry,' she said slowly, her eyes still closed. I looked at her so vulnerable and lovely.

'Sorry Anita, you're not choking on your own vomit,' and heaved her up, she was probably about eight stone but getting her up was hard.

'You nice boy nice to me.'

I looked for her bedroom, then half dragged her there and laid her on the bed, taking off her shoes. I could see a dressing gown behind the door and draped it over her and the flat was warm so she would be alright. I got a glass of water, looked for some aspirin but couldn't see any but thought surely four Babychams can't be that bad anyway?

You're a nice person, Frankie,' and looked up at me, her face all smudged and almost crying. She put her arms up in the air and I thought for a moment before I put them back down.

I laughed at the absurdity of it all, sighed and smoothed her hair away from her eyes. I left a note by the water glass with a taxi number, planted a kiss on her forehead and left.

At ten o'clock the next day Anita was still not in, I had rung her flat but there was no answer. I was thinking about whether I should drive round when the phone rang. I could tell it was an outside line; I heard pips as someone put money into a payphone.

'Frank, it's me, I'm sorry about last night, I'm still not really sure what I said or did…'

'You were fine you were funny actually, you didn't embarrass yourself,' I laughed.

'Well, I have now. I'm at the pub and my car is on bricks.'

I laughed uproariously.

'It's not funny, it's literally on bricks,' said Anita.

'What the wheels have been nicked?'

'Yes.'

'Ok. Ok. Let me think. I'll call Ryder's and they'll recover it for you; I'll tell Bill what's happened, I've got a meeting now so you'll have to get a taxi into work. Ok? See you in half an hour.'

The pips cut the public box phone off.

Eric, the IRM, had called a meeting to discuss the implications of the engineering unions calling a national UK-wide strike and potential effects on production. I arrived late and whispered what had happened with Anita to Bill.

Eric was in his understated talking mode,

'It's an indefinite two day a week strike, the AEUW and EETPU craft unions are involved. It looks like it's shut Rolls

Royce aero completely, but we're not in the Engineering Employers' Federation pay negotiations so formally we're not affected. However, as many of our car parts come from EEF companies we may be hit by secondary action.'

There was a silence while this sank in. Bill asked the first question,

'I thought Jim Prior in the new government was saying secondary action would not be possible…'

Jim cut across him with,

'My wife is more worried there's no *Corrie* because of the ITV strike.'

Everyone laughed.

Eric continued,

'Bill's made a good point and we have someone lobbying Government right now trying to find out the secondary picket situation. We're also worried about the possible steel industry national strike. The unions are opposed to the importation of cheaper coking coal, but of course the reduction in steel price would be good for us. But with oil just having gone up to $18 a barrel the environment is getting very tough indeed.'

He puffed his pipe and continued steadily on,

'Our pay claim is due this week; if its anything like the 45% ITV staff are demanding we are in real trouble.'

I looked around, no one seemed about to speak so I asked, 'The CBI seems to be opposing the government-proposed changes to union laws in case it antagonises the unions, is our management supporting the CBI position?'

Eric stared, 'Good question Frank. Yes, it is a contradiction as clearly, we are a closed shop employer. Head office personnel are looking at where we should be on this issue, I can't say any more right now.'

I smiled. So, the company management might be lobbying the new government to retain the ridiculous damaging closed shop. What a joke I thought. For once I kept my thoughts private.

We split up and went back to our offices, Anita was waiting for me bedraggled and soaked through from the rain.

'Coffee and a Marathon bar for the hero,' and handed them to me.

'Wow, I'm honoured,' trying not to laugh at her appearance.

'You can be honest, what did I say... I know I was a disgrace...' as she brushed her tangled hair.

'Nothing, nothing at all you were mumbling but quite nice, just avoid Babycham on an empty stomach,' and bit my lips.

'Why don't I believe you?' she said looking at me intently for the first time. I looked away.

'Listen, I'll go to the PTA briefing meeting and you sort out the best way for us to get to London then.'

'Ok, and thanks by the way.' She stood up and backed out of the door, all the time keeping her eyes on my face.

— 21 —

Club

The autumn turned into winter, and I was pleased that the BL staff had finally refused to go on strike for the reinstatement of the sacked Red Robbo. It looked like they were still no nearer to accepting the pay offer, so it was unclear how far they had morphed into finally accepting Michael Edwards' 'streamlining plan'.

Reading the papers at home, I could see how extensively the backbench Tory MPs were criticising the Employment Secretary, Jim Prior. They were calling him out as 'soft on unions' and even the Ford Chairman was in the papers castigating the British Ford factories for 'intransigence to change.' He was extensively quoted as saying that some jobs were taking half as much time again in Britain as on the Continent, though as he was a sales guy with no responsibility for manufacturing, I wasn't convinced he would actually know the truth of that statement.

Later that evening, I met Pete in the usual wine bar in Aigburth and both of us were looking forward to a good argument about politics. Pete was pleased the BL staff had not accepted the 'derisory 5%' they were being offered in the pay claim, even when I read out from the *Mail* that there were four months' stocks of BL vehicles, so layoffs were almost guaranteed.

After a few pints I was getting animated, I was losing patience yet again with Pete's approach to labour relations,

'It's not Edwards or Red Robbo who will do for the BL factories you idiot, it's the bloody customer – no one wants an Allegro,' I shouted after a few beers. 'Audi have just released a 4WD Quattro, top speed of 137 mph – that's the future not the bloody Allegro.'

Pete was always at his weakest arguing about the car industry as I had inside knowledge; I was on a roll and carried on. I knew Pete was a keen motorcyclist.

'And who wants a 1960's technology Norton Commando either, have you seen the new Honda 750 four or the Kawasaki 2 stroke triples...'

'Oh, shut up...' said Pete and then we were interrupted by a sudden shriek.

'Mr Thomas, how are you? Tina, this is him he's dead nice.'

I looked up, startled to see Stella from the canteen, dressed like a mild punk in short black skirt woolly tights and Dr. Martens boots, with an equally good-looking friend. She sat straight in my lap without asking, and I was forced to put my arm round her to stop her falling off. She whispered into my ear, 'I gorrit!'

'The house?' I replied. I had helped her ensure her payslips supported the mortgage she needed.

'Yeah. I'm over the moon.'

She held my head in both hands and planted a big kiss on my lips.

'We're goin' to a club to celebrate, are you coming?'

'Well, Stella...' I said before Pete interrupted, 'You're on, definitely.'

'Tina will gerrus in, her brother's the bouncer.'

Stella stood up and took my hand to help me up, and then placed it round her waist, I didn't object. Her last words to me that time she left the office came back, *Everybody is looking for something Mr Thomas.'*

I looked at her and grinned, she was wearing heavy black Bowie-type makeup that I'd only seen in London before. Make up seemed a definite must for scouse girls on a night out. Her friend Tina had grabbed Pete by the arm, and we left the wine bar and headed towards the club.

Tina had got us nodded through. The noise was stupendous, I could not understand a word the girls said, lip-reading was about it. We were immediately dancing a foursome to 'Sheena is a Punk Rocker' by the Ramones. At the end of the song, Stella jumped on me wrapped both legs round and gave me a long lingering French kiss. I was literally gobsmacked. Two hours later we all ended up back in Tina's flat, next to Sefton Park a short walk from the club.

On the way back to the car the next day, Pete said that he'd arranged to meet Tina on Sunday.

'I wish I wasn't moving to London now with the new job,' he said wistfully.

'Well, Stella won't be going on Sunday, she's got a young son to look after. It was a great night though bloody fantastic,' I acknowledged.

'I might transfer to the car industry if all the staff are as funny as them,' Pete said.

At 9 a.m. Monday morning, I was in an anteroom at the Liverpool Industrial Tribunal court rooms, a surprisingly modern building for a Victorian city centre. There were eight of us from the management side for the PTA shop steward dismissal case and it had yet to start. We waited patiently, we knew their barrister and the PTA IRM were in discussions with the trade union side solicitor. I had my crib-notes in my pocket, the PTA POs had whiteboards, maps and huge folders of evidence. The barrister emerged, sharp featured with an aquiline nose.

'Right, listen up everybody,' like we were in the military,

'I have here a signed resignation letter and confidentiality agreement which includes the company paying a fixed sum of maintenance for three years while the plaintiff does a degree at Liverpool Uni.'

'What the hell!' exclaimed one of the POs in disbelief.

'The case is now settled out of court so there will be no tribunal, you are free to go back to work,' continued the barrister.

'We had him bang to rights, it's a bloody sell out,' said one of the POs.

I was shocked, it wasn't even the plant I worked in, but I was pissed off given the effort we had put into dismissing him. I got up amidst the confusion and went to a public phone to ring Anita.

'Hi, it's Frank. You'll never guess what, he's resigned and is going to uni for three years at our expense.'

'So, there is no IT then?' queried Anita.

'No, we're having a coffee than back to work at some stage apparently. The Assembly Plant POs are well pissed, they wanted their pound of flesh. Will you nip along and tell Bill what's happened for me?'

'Sure, I will. We'll be in the canteen at one o'clock if you want to tell us about it,' she added.

The pips started, sounding for more coins; I said, 'The assembly boys are organising a hotel lunch, so I won't be back in time, bye,' and hung up. (They weren't, but I really didn't want to see Anita at the moment.)

I drove back out of the city towards the factory. The decline of the docks was so palpable that some of the warehouses had never been repaired since wartime bombing; scrapyards and under the arches dodgy businesses abounded. Toxteth looked bleak, even in the weak winter sun. Sefton Park with the faded glory of huge Victorian houses was nicely reflected. I knew I had no answers, but I hoped that at least Thatcher would help business get a grip on the plague of industrial action that was hastening the inner-city decline. Could anyone seriously contemplate opening a business in Liverpool in 1979?

The national steel strike was on the midday news, the steel unions were talking about picketing car and parts factories. This was apparently because they were 'importing private steel'. Yet the same item said state controlled British Steel produced only 122 tonnes per hour, compared with German Thyssen's 370 tonnes per hour and Japanese Nippon's 520 tonnes per hour. I shouted 'right on' when the journalist said Jim Prior was being called 'Pussyfoot Prior' because of his reluctance to get to grips with secondary picketing. However, I still wondered how long it would be before Thatcher did a Ted Heath 'U turn'; with interest rates at 17%, she seemed powerless.

I was depressed both by the ridiculous tribunal deal and the news, so decided on the spur of the moment to drive into my flat's car park rather than carry on back to work. After all, I was supposed to be out all day, and no one was expecting me back. As I walked up the stairs, I was thinking about the news comment that Britain was the 'sick man of Europe' on the radio. I knew from being around Liverpudlians that there was humour in everything and smiled to myself about the week's *Fawlty Towers* episode on TV where the American tourist had said, 'I'm suggesting this is the crummiest, shoddiest hotel in Europe,' to which the Major replied, 'No, no, there's that place in Eastbourne.'

It summed up the state of the country for me. I made a coffee with my new Habitat cafetiere and sat back looking over the car park at the back of the flats, feet up on the cracked Formica table. I knew I'd a melancholic personality, prone to introspection and that's why I liked listening to Leonard Cohen (ok, occasionally Joni Mitchell). I thought over the volatile six months that had just ended. I was still surprised by the attitude to work of many of the operators. The poor timekeeping, the welt working, the extended tea breaks and the indifference to union militancy. Granted, I'd painfully learnt that some of the managers and foremen were no better; for God's sake, there were three or even four different canteens for different grades of staff. Talk about 'them and us', but many of the managers just accepted poor quality work and seemed to have no balls to sort out the poor performers. I realised a few of the senior managers were good; I thought one or two were visionaries who could see how the British-based car industry was going the way of the motorcycle and truck industry.

But they all seemed powerless to influence events. Even the Thatcherite politicians who I'd high hopes were going to turn things round, had little impact other than getting a European rebate. Industrial relations were no different than they were under the last Labour administration. Maybe I was naive, maybe I was too young, and maybe I cared too much.

Maybe I just needed to accept perennial underachievement. Eight months of the Tories and they were still propping up British Steel and British Leyland.

It was getting darker, I'd made myself thoroughly miserable and what about my love life? It seemed to reflect the state of the country, false promises and false starts, with nothing much delivered. I sat there; I knew I'd personally tried so hard to make a difference at work. I'd taken not inconsiderable risks with the flag burner, the diabetic, the sick pad men, even with Stella and her mortgage. But what real difference did I make if the factory went on just the same?

And Anita, Anita, I muttered to myself.

I lay down on the sofa and dozed off, Leonard Cohen's *Death of a Ladies' Man* playing on the cassette tape player.

— 22 —

Pay Claim

Lenny Lobo walked in, shutting the door behind him.

'Pre-production version, for me bessie mate.'

'What?' I said.

'This year's pay claim, whadda you think?'

I put out my hand, but Lenny refused to hand it over.

'Write it down, wuzz.' He read it out, haltingly.

'The chairman said we made $100 million last year, and even though there was a nine-week pay strike our productivity is up on the year before and he's got an 80% pay increase.'

I was sceptical but continued writing on my A4 pad.

'The Tory government bastards…' I looked up… 'Ok it doesn't say that, but they've scrapped price controls so school dinners, rates, gas, prescriptions are all up. Inflation is now at 16% and expected 20% at year-end.' He stuttered, 'Oh, and our beloved German workers have five weeks holiday to our four and we want pensions at sixty and a thirty-five-hour week.'

I looked down at my notes,

'So what percentage increase is that then?'

Lenny looked at the note,

'Don't know, it just says £30 a week on basic wage.'

I got out my calculator, 'Thanks, give us a copy then.'

'Fuck off, you've had yuh lot.' He got up to leave, 'You owe me one Frank.'

'Bugger off and do some work for once,' and we both laughed as he left.

I wandered down to Bill's office. He never looked up, whoever came in.

'Have you seen the pay claim yet?'

Bill glanced up, from his paperwork.

'Have you, where is it?

'A steward just read it out to me verbatim...' he put his hand up and cut across me.

He picked up his phone,

'June. Get Eric in London on the speaker phone right now, tell him it's urgent.'

It rang almost instantly,

'Eric, I've got Frank in my office, a steward has read out a verbatim copy of the pay claim just now.'

'Did he now? We're not getting it till four o'clock this afternoon so spit it out laddie.'

I read out my notes.

'Brilliant. Good work, we need to be a bit more prepared on the chairman's salary, knowing that. Who was the steward?'

'I'd rather not say, but he's reliable,' I said.

'Ok. Did he say who signed it?'

'Yeah, the lead T and G negotiator,'

'Great thanks, good work that,' and clicked off.

Bill looked at me.

'I hope you're not doing dodgy deals now; why did he read it to you?' raising his eyebrows and lighting up a cigarette.

'What do you think?' I said slightly annoyed. 'Do you think we'll be back on security duties again?' Bill thought for a moment,

'I can't see the company conceding much of that claim, but it may depend on this new Tory anti-union stuff, that could be a game changer. The way Maggie is standing up to Europe anything is possible, I can see why the Soviets are calling her the "Iron Lady". Most of our staff are still skint from last year's strike, they'll do absolutely anything to avoid another strike. Umm, ok on your way, good work as Eric said.'

He put his head down to his paperwork, always a sign that a meeting was over.

The following Monday I was in early, as I knew the poxy body in white line manning issue was still not resolved. There was a handwritten note from Lenny Lobo on my desk waiting for me with a list of bullet point issues requiring sorting before they would even re-enter discussions on manning levels. I read the note carefully:

* Gap between car body and door rack line too narrow.
* Platforms online brazing station need lowering.
* Lower back panel man has no work area for tools.
* Tool locker needed for spring man toolbox.
* No emergency stops inner feed.
* Overhead airlines too close to car.

I felt seriously pissed off. All of these would require electrical and mechanical fitting work, all would be costly. In the management meeting later that day, I argued they were just excuses and the company should do none of them. I was surprised when I was overruled and they were agreed to. To me, it was just an excuse for management not to press the issue. Pathetic.

Two days later a trial of the slightly reduced manning was started, so I went out to have a look at it. It all seemed to be going ok, so I went back to my office. Thirty minutes later, the line was stopped due to an accident. No one had seen it, but a brazer appeared to have been caught in his tool line while crossing the production line and was concussed.

Lenny appeared, standing at the door,

'Youse had yuh chips, we're not touching it till the factory inspector gets in,' and left.

The whole plant was completely stopped, no production at all. The factory inspector duly arrived and after 200 cars were lost in the time that took, declared it a hazard, so the crossover brazer position would have to be reorganised. The maximum theoretical saving was now three men per shift. Another complete waste of time, with huge effort involved. Without leaving any messages, I upped sticks walked out and drove home. I just couldn't stand another minute in the factory.

Racialism

One drab afternoon, George Tolley, a car body sides foreman appeared at the door of my office, gleeful like he'd won the football pools.

'I've got Marley the smoked Irishman, he's been leaving the factory early and getting someone else to clock him out.'

Irked by his language, I looked up at the old-fashioned, loudmouthed supervisor.

'Did you miss the Race Relations Act training day then? Eh? Just suspend him and we'll have the disciplinary hearing at nine o'clock tomorrow,' I said.

'Yeah, I did I was off sick. I'll be glad to see the back of him, he's probably a dope head too,' he continued.

'And do you have any evidence for that?' I said.

'No but…'

'Then forget it and go and get your clocking evidence properly sorted. See you tomorrow morning and close the door on the way out.'

Five minutes later, as if by magic, Lenny Lobo, appeared.

'Err, Frank my son, this Bob Marley case…'

'Is that really his name?' I laughed.

'Yeah, he changed it by deed poll. I can't stand the lad personally like, but he's been here three years and gets on with the job in a world of his own like. No one will have clocked for him, he's Billie no mates I tell yuh. The lads say Tolley's a bit of a racialist, he's said nowt to me like, he knows I'd hang one on him, but that's what they say.'

I looked at Lenny for a moment,

'So, you want me to take a closer look at the evidence then?

'Yeah, you're catching on, son.'

As Lenny left, I muttered to myself, 'I wish I was.' We had come to an understanding that he would let me know if he was unhappy with the likely outcome of any upcoming disciplinary hearing, after an absurd dispute that had lost twenty-four cars. This was only the second time he had alluded to the understanding in ten months.

As 'wrongful clocking' was a potential gross misconduct dismissal for fraud, the following day's meeting was chaired by the area superintendent, a manager who looked after 300 men of the 5000 in the car factory. George Tolley the foreman, Lenny Lobo, the union steward, Bob Marley and me as the local personnel officer were also present. Worryingly, there was no senior site union convenor; he would normally attend potential dismissals. He could be absent because he thought Lenny was experienced enough to handle it or because he didn't really care if the guy was dismissed. I was nervous as to which it might be.

Marley looked like a proper Brixton Rastafarian with the dreadlocks, yellow and green jumper and tea cosy hat. I grinned as I had seen the real Bob Marley at a concert in Birmingham in 1977.

The superintendent and I sat on one side of his desk with the others seated opposite. After introductions, he invited Tolley to start proceedings.

'I was looking for Mr Marley for fifteen minutes before clocking off time at the end of the morning shift yesterday. I wanted to ask him if he'd like to work overtime Saturday. I stood by the clocking machine from 1.45 to 2.00 pm but didn't see him, yet I found his card clocked at 2.00 pm on later inspection. This proved to me he'd already left the site and an unknown workmate had falsely clocked him out.'

We all looked at Marley for a response.

'No consternation. I had a case of the runs and worked five cars back up the production line before a long toilet break, after which I clocked out normally. I've explained this twice now.'

Lenny the steward turned to question Marley.

'Bob, isn't it, I'm told by the lads that youse are mad enough to enjoy working here?

'Love it man, simple work, its nirvana. I allow my mind to travel all over the things that are good in ma life,' Marley said in a Birmingham accent.

'And do youse ever work overtime cos I've never seen you do any,' said Lenny.

'No, never done a day in ma life, am surprised he look for me to ask as I never done it man and said never would,' Marley replied.

I scribbled away. I would have to produce notes from the meeting whatever the outcome, and then it was my turn to ask questions.

'George, have you questioned his workmates about anyone clocking him out that day?'

Lenny butted in. 'Err I always advise my members not to cooperate with the management on these things, there's been confrontations about who saw what and where; we never take no part in your disciplinary investigations,' he stated.

I shrugged but continued anyway,

'So, the only evidence is that you stood by the clocking station and never saw him clock out?'

'Yep' said Tolley.

We argued round the houses for a while longer about the importance of witnesses when it's one man's word against the others. The superintendent lost patience and called an adjournment, and everyone left the room except for the two of us.

The superintendent, an Irishman transferred from the Dagenham plant said, 'Well, I guess I'm supporting the foreman here. On the balance of probabilities Marley has fiddled his clock.'

'I can't agree,' I said. 'He's been here three years now, he's got no record of any misdemeanours at all, he says he loves his job and the steward says he's no friends who would risk their jobs to clock him out. Likelihood is Tolley missed him if he really was standing there every minute.'

He looked at me, unconvinced by my argument. 'Can we get Tolley in on his own and ask him some more questions in private?' I ventured.

The superintendent looked at his watch, reluctantly agreed and called everyone back into the office. He said he wished to make some further enquiries with Mr Tolley and that they should all reconvene same time tomorrow. This was rare in a disciplinary meeting, as it usually implied management and personnel did not agree.

We brought Tolley the foreman back in on his own. I went straight for it.

'George, some of your lads have said they've heard you making racialist comments in the tearoom, is that true?' I opened.

'Rubbish, who said that? I'll bloody batter them…'

'I'll take that as a "no" shall I? So, how are you so sure you didn't miss him at the clock? There must have been fifty blokes queuing?' I said.

'Cos he's as black as coal – it'd be hard to miss that twat.'

I stared open-mouthed.

'So, you don't like black people then is it?' I said.

Tolley stood up slowly, hands on the desk, glowering,

'I never said I didn't like coloureds. I've had enough of this, you're a snotty nosed trainee in personnel calling me a liar when I'm just trying to do my job. I'm not having it, I'm getting my own union rep to take part in this, it's me you're judging now for just doing my job.' He turned and left, leaving the Superintendent and me looking at each other, nonplussed.

Irritated that I was still a graduate trainee for another month, I went back to my office to make a start on the meeting notes. Not five minutes later, my boss Bill glided into the office shutting the door, a bad sign.

'I've just had the white-collar supervisor's union rep in my office, making a formal complaint about your questioning of George Tolley. He said you called him a racialist liar?'

I looked hard at Bill. He was my mentor and someone I respected enormously,

'Not so, I suggested he could have missed him at the clocking station and asked him what he thought of some of his staff saying he was racialist.'

'Frank, that's well out of order saying that with no evidence, you know that. Right, here's what we are gonna do. I'll chair the reconvened meeting tomorrow and you can take the notes. The foreman's union is threatening industrial action because personnel are not supporting management in this case. I have never seen this before, we could really do without it.'

I was brassed off. After ten months in the job, I had a feel for what I thought was baloney, and with the self-righteousness of youth, never hesitated to say.

'Do without what, trying to find the facts?'

Bill ignored my question and stood up to leave, clearly annoyed with me. Lenny appeared again,

'I can see youse got a cob on. I'll tell you something else. I've asked around again and there is defo no one that would risk their own job to clock him out. That foreman's got it in for him, cos he's half-caste.'

I desperately wanted to tell Lenny I agreed with him for once but couldn't.

'Look, I'll be honest with yuh. Rumour is, some of the daft lads we have here, are taking their protective gear off on nights and Marley won't cooperate with 'em.'

'Why?' I said.

'He's a discer, they sand off the lead joins between the roof and the body sides…'

'I know what they do, Lenny.'

'They get shite money, like dirt money for lead dust contamination of the lungs and they don't wanna lose it. When they see a nurse with a clipboard, they wear the protective gear, but like on nightshift they try not to wear it but Marley still does.'

'So, he's the sensible one and his mates don't like it?'

'Yeah, the Company Doctor is getting suspicious of the monitoring results and the lads blame Marley for not playing along. I'm just tellin' you why no one would ever clock him out and risk their own jobs. You keep that dust stuff to yourself, you hear?'

'For God's sake, this factory is a bloody joke,' I said.

After he'd left, I thought for a minute before deciding to ring my college friend Pete who worked at a left-wing labour think tank to ask him for a favour. He had said something to me about his network of 'sympathetic insiders' the week before when we had met up for a drink. As I put down the phone, Jim, sidled in smirking,

'Is it true you're standing in the way of Rasta man getting his cards?' he said.

'Can't say Jim, it's confidential,' and smiled back.

'I've got a cousin in the white-collar union, they're goin' to hang you out to dry if you don't support the foreman,' he said quietly out of the corner of his mouth.

'Are they now? Well, they can all sod off, I'll recommend what I think is right,' I said.

I got up, opened the door for Jim to leave and turned off the strip fluorescent lights, turning on the Anglepoise desk light I'd brought from my flat. This usually helped my headaches when I was tense.

Anita, then made an appearance. She was seriously nosy.

'Christ, it's like Piccadilly Circus in here today.'

'What?' she said.

I noticed the faint whiff of perfume and newly styled hair. I'd still not heard whether she was accepting her new job offer.

'So, you're the talk of the factory as word is you called a supervisor a racist?'

'And?'

'I can see you're upset Frank, you're grinding your teeth. I've come to say that there's actually going to be a motion at the supervisor's union for all the foremen to stop working with you.' I stared at her, shocked at the news,

'Let them then. If senior management support them rather than me, I'll resign, simple. Bugger the lot of them, sorry,' I said.

'Have you got some kind of martyr complex?' Anita said.

'Yeah, I'm a martyr to us running disciplinary meetings fairly, not accepting the lies of a racist bigot.'

'Do you have any evidence he's a racist?' said Anita calmly.

'No.'

'Frank, I'm just trying to help. You said nothing to anyone about my pub embarrassment and I'm just returning the favour.' I shook my head,

'I don't want any favours returned thanks.' I was pissed off she could even think helping her out of the previous pub episode was a 'favour' that needed returning.

'You're difficult to talk to when you're like this,' she said.

'It takes one to know one though, doesn't it?' She rolled her eyes,

'Look, do you want to go for a drink after work tonight to discuss this mess?' she suggested. It was complicated, I knew I would love to go for a drink with her, but after the false starts and her saying she was leaving the job I was reluctant to even think about seeing her again, even if I did value her opinions.

'It's not a mess as you call it. Thanks, but no thanks, I need to prepare for tomorrow, it might be my last day in personnel if everyone who's been in here today is right.' I said wearily.

'Why don't you try the glass half full approach?' she asked.

'Because the glass isn't even bloody here today that's why,' I replied. I felt a mess, five o'clock shadow from my crap electric razor, bags under my eyes and sweating into an unironed shirt.

'I'll be at the Black Bull in Gateacre at six o'clock tonight then, for half an hour. If you don't turn up, I'll take it personally,' and smiling she got up and went back next door.

I picked up my work papers, drove home to my flat and stood in the kitchen with angry black clouds running fast across the sky. The company press cuttings were so depressing they actually cheered me up for once. Vauxhall flying pickets were blockading Harwich and Felixstowe ports to prevent parts for their cars coming into the country! I laughed at the piece in the *Telegraph,* about a pet shop owner who had bought an automatic Austin Princess after the TV 'Buy British' campaign. It had printed the words he'd used to complain about the car in court: 'It groaned, grunted, rattled and knocked.' More seriously, right after this, the paper quoted the letter from the BL car company Chairman to all staff: 'How can we persuade a Conservative government to give us funds to secure our recovery when union officials are bent on thwarting our plans?'

How indeed, such was the ridiculous nature of manufacturing in 1979 Britain? My thoughts drifted back to Anita's offer of meeting up; it was quite brave of her to be seen in a pub where she had got blind drunk and had her car wheels nicked in the car park. The irony of it made me smile, so I sniffed under my arms sprayed on Brut 33 and decided I would walk along to the pub for two drinks maximum. Whether I would actually have a personnel job tomorrow might possibly depend on my college friend Pete coming up with the goods...

Anita was in the same seat as last time. The barmaid recognised me and pointed in her direction stifling a laugh. I ordered a pint of Higson's and went over to where she was sitting but sat opposite rather than next to her.

'The barmaid asked if I had my new wheels yet,' she laughed, which eased the tension. 'So?'

'So what?' I said, determined to be cool. I looked at her again and had a terrible thought,

'Has the boss sent you to tell me to apologise to Tolley for what I said?'

Anita frowned,

'I haven't seen Bill for the last two days, all I know is what the supervisors have said about things.'

'Well, we know there's no confidentiality in personnel, don't we?' I had another gulp and stood up, 'I'm having another one, can I get you anything?'

'Yes, a Pepsi and a packet of pork scratchings... no, make it crisps,' she said mischievously. I grinned at the reference to a previous faux pas. The pub had a funny mix of shop workers from over the road, managers and secretaries, with a few well-heeled retired looking people thrown in. I looked again, it was a proper community pub, and I wasn't sure why I didn't come more regularly. It was probably the old-fashioned stuffed animals on every wall that put me off.

I sat down again and too tired to put my brain in gear said, 'I thought you were leaving?'

She stared back at me. 'I've turned it down, it's tough here but I'm still learning a lot, so I said no. What do they say, whatever doesn't kill you makes you stronger?' I was disappointed I didn't get a mention in her decision process but was past that now.

'Glad to hear it,' I replied

'Are you?' For once, I didn't fill the silence and sat there. Eventually, I said, 'You never said what happened that weekend you went home to see your fiancé?'

'You never asked me,' Anita replied looking directly at me. After a long pause, she said, 'It's history, I said an arranged marriage was not going to happen and that I was not giving up my career full stop. Ever since, my mum has stopped talking to me as she says I've caused the family a loss of face in our community.'

'Oh,' was all I could say, surprised by her frankness.

'You know, my Dad said to me a true friend is one that always tells the truth.'

'Sounds ominous,' I said drinking nervously.

'It's well known you care more about the bloody car factory, and the people who work there, than the rest of us put together,' she sat forward but continued, 'I admit for me, this job is just a tick in the box for my CV. Industrial relations experience in one of the toughest sites in the country...' Anita paused. Feigning indifference, I said,

'And?'

'It will be a tragedy if you throw it all away tomorrow, because if you're blacked by the supervisors' union you'll end up in some training backwater...'

'That's where you're wrong. I won't, I'll just leave. I know what I've have tried to do for ten months in this job; if my view on this case isn't acceptable to senior management so be it.'

'You sound like some hippie fatalist as well as a martyr,' she replied quickly. 'Are you expecting the blue-collar union to come charging over the hill to rescue you from the white-collar union, because the union convenor doesn't care whether Marley goes or stays. Can you not see that?'

'I've no illusions about trade union politics or racism. If I lose, I lose. The case stinks, and I'm not going along with it even if the convenor is. Anyway, I've gotta go and prepare so I'll see you tomorrow.'

Before I could stand up, Anita grabbed my hand across the table.

'Don't throw your career away, Frank.' I frowned but liked the concern in her eyes. I shook myself free and walked out.

The next day, the disciplinary meeting was in my boss Bill's conference size office. Two conference rooms nearby were being used as ante rooms, one for Tolley and his staff union representative, and one for Marley and Lenny, his union rep. The stage was set, as much as it ever could be in a Liverpool car factory.

Bill opened the meeting by saying that as there was some difference of opinion about the facts of the case, he would be chairing the meeting rather than the superintendent, with a fresh perspective. He summarised my notes and asked if there were any further thoughts or comments since the day before.

The foreman's staff union representative, a grumpy looking older man in his sixties looked at me directly,

'It feels to our side, that there has not been the proper personnel support of a supervisor trying to do a difficult job to the best of his ability. I'm here just to ensure we see no more of that today.'

I sat feeling surly for a moment and then said I would like to ask Tolley a question. I could see Bill's eyes rise with a frown. This was not in his script for running the meeting.

'George, would you describe the National Front as a racialist organisation?'

'What's that got to do with clocking?' His voice was beginning to sound angry. The white-collar union representative cut across,

'I warned you, and that's a question that has nothing to do with a clocking dispute, it's ridiculous and we are not…'

Bill put up his hand,

'Frank, what exactly is your point?'

'My information is that George is a member of the Liverpool branch of the National Front, a self-confessed racialist organisation and that Mr Marley is self-evidently black…'

The foreman's union rep interrupted shouting,

'That's an outrageous slur and we're not bloody having it…'

'Why don't you just answer the question George,' I shouted back, looking at Tolley.

Bill stood up, 'Right, I'm calling an adjournment so we can all cool down, please go back to your rooms until I come and get you.'

When they had left, Bill looked at me,

'Frank, that was completely and utterly out…'

I waved a piece of paper above my head,

'I have a signed copy here of his membership form, look at it. He's a member of a probable fascist organisation and we are expected to believe his word against a black guy with no witnesses…' Bill took the paper, looking carefully at the form, visibly sighing. He passed it to the superintendent.

'Right ok. Ok. Ok. For God's sake. What a mess. Look, I'm still not going down any racist route here, even if he is a member of the NF. This does not prove Tolley is lying. I'm just going to say there is, there is, umm, no corroborating evidence for the alleged clocking incident and that we will give Marley the benefit of the doubt this time.'

The superintendent, who was the owning line manager of Marley said,

'Bill, if you accept this, the supervisors' union will know why the case was thrown out, so…'

'I can't control that, but they may not want to actually say that of course, for reasons of their own.' I wasn't sure what Bill meant by that but was feeling relieved that it looked like Marley was not being dismissed after all. Bill called the other participants back in. They sat there quietly and after a while Bill spoke.

'Management has decided, having listened to all the evidence, not to proceed with disciplinary action on this occasion based on insufficient evidence. However, Mr Marley needs to be more careful about his toilet habits near clocking off time.'

Tolley and his rep stared at each other, stood up and left, abruptly followed by Lenny Lobo and Marley slapping each other on the back.

The superintendent said nothing, got up to go but said to me as he opened the door to leave, 'How did you get a copy of that membership form then?

'A friend,' I said. As soon as the door closed, Bill stared at me,

'What an embarrassment that was. You should have shown me that form before we started, this is not some kind of fucking theatre. That membership form must have been obtained illegally and so the company could be in all sorts of trouble if Tolley takes this further. We are probably vicariously liable for you using it. Christ, what a cockup. You haven't heard the last of this, and you of all people.'

I was unashamedly unrepentant, 'But it stopped a probably racialist foreman unfairly dismissing someone…'

Bill cut across, 'You can't accuse someone of being a racialist in…'

'I didn't… I just asked him if he was a member of the National Front.'

'You're a bloody maverick Frank. You know you should have cleared a controversial question like that with me before you asked it,' said Bill.

I stared back,

'Are we now investigating Tolley for lying then?' I said, regretting it as soon as the words came out, realising there was no evidence he had lied.

Bill stood up collected his papers and left. On the way out I shouted, 'I'll write the notes up out of your way this afternoon.'

I sat still for a moment, exhausted. I went upstairs to look for a quiet room to write the notes and found one with a long oak table. The silence away from the factory was overwhelming. Although I was pleased with the result, I knew I didn't have any real evidence of direct racialism and that I was just lucky my friend had access to some damning information. It could just be an honest mistake, but then Tolley would be judged by the company he kept. There was a knock, Bill put his head round the door.

'Just to say the white-collar union want a meeting about how future clocking offences should be handled in the light of today's "no corroborating evidence" conclusion. Surprise, surprise, you are not invited but make sure you let me see the notes before you issue them. Did you hear that last bit?'

'Yes, no problem,' I replied as Bill left. So, it wasn't over yet for me. I looked out of the second-floor window towards the Speke Road and across to the council estate. It was not unlike the one I grew up on, except the River Mersey was in the far distance beyond. I stewed in my own juice for a while, but unable to summon any enthusiasm for writing the notes I decided to go home and do them there.

As I opened the flat door, the phone was ringing.

'Right Frank, err, Lenny here, I'm ringing from the steward's office. I'm on afternoons like two till ten tonight...'

'Lenny, I know what afternoons are.'

'Is Anita yer best tart then?'

'What?' I said.

'Yer know, yer future Judy like?'

'What the hell are you goin' on about Lenny?' I said.

'Well, she was in the tearoom askin' about youse earlier.'

'Go on then.'

'I heard a load of catcallin' and monkey noises and then she strolled into the tearoom in van body sides framing I'm tellin' yuh. The lads were half naked without their weldin' leathers like. She wanted a private word about what happened today. I took her next door to the training room and said ask Bill, he was there but she said he was pissed off and saying nothin' like.'

'Go on Lenny.'

'She was worried you'd been hot headed and were gonna be blacked by the blockermen's union, so I put her straight. I told her you'd embarrassed the foreman, saved Marley from the parish, I mean dismissal and the foreman's union now knows Tolley is a racist twat. Listen, I gotta go, I'm doin' a toilet relief for someone now, but I thought you needed to know. Are you sure she's not yuh best tart?'

'On yer bike Lenny, and thanks for ringing.'

Thinking about the day's ever stranger events I decided to go for a pint to read the newspapers and clear my head before starting the boring job of writing the meeting notes. I ordered two pints of bitter at the same time, knowing the first would be gone in a few minutes so the second one wouldn't go flat. I picked 'Anita's seat' and sat there with the newspapers. Before I opened them, I realised I was flattered that Anita had cared enough to go and talk to Lenny. The papers were full of the usual strike stuff. Foden Trucks in Sandbach, who were not on strike, were announcing redundancies anyway. Vauxhall Cars at Ellesmere Port were still on strike and Talbot Cars Ryton thirteen-week strike was at last over. I was amused to see an unusual story over the Mersey. The Champion spark plugs plant at Upton on the Wirral had sixty women cross through violent picket lines to get to their machines, despite being threatened with dismissal. That was a brave first, as to lose your union card in a closed shop meant losing your job. To cap it all, a supervisor and seventeen paint shop workers at the Range Rover body plant in Birmingham had been caught sleeping on nightshift. Seventeen. Maybe our Company manning standards were not that slack after all.

I decided to have one more then go home via the local Chinese for a takeaway. Despite the positive outcome, there was one personal issue that was still nagging me so I started to write on a beer mat. The heading was 'pros and cons of leaving this job'.

I looked up when I heard the barmaid say, 'Do you take it in turns?'

'Sorry?'

I followed the barmaid's eyes and could dimly make out Anita through the tobacco fug.

'Hello Frank, I thought you might be here,' she said breezily.

I looked up at her, putting the beer mat in my top pocket. I stared at my watch and looked up again.

'Anita?' I said slowly. 'What are you doing here, we didn't arrange to meet did we?'

'No, I'm not stopping. I just came to tell you you have a nine o'clock meeting. Bill has called a meeting for all of us about clocking policy,' I looked at the time again.

'Tomorrow, not tonight!' I looked into her liquid, dark eyes and sighed.

'Anita.'

'Frank,' she replied amused.

'Are you on your own, has Bill sent you?'

'No, why would he? What have you done?' she asked.

'I honestly don't know,' I replied. I was embarrassed about Lenny earlier calling her 'my best tart'. I stood up, knocking into the table,

'I've gotta go,' and then sat down again, as if I had forgotten to say something important.

'Anita, why are you here?' I asked,

'Oh, I just came to see you are ok after today.'

' I'm not ok, I've over-imbibed as Churchill would have said.'

'Really? I would never have guessed it,' she said. I got up again, she helped move the table, so I didn't knock it and steadied my arm. I gently shrugged her off and walked unsteadily towards the door, stopping as I met the cold air from outside.

'Come on, I'll give you a lift to your flat,' she offered.

'No, it's a mess I don't want you to, to see it. I'll walk thanks. I have to write the notes of the Marley meeting up tonight.'

'Come on get in, I won't look in your flat I'll drop you outside.'

I carried on, then turned round and waved, a little unsteady but not drunk. She was still standing there, she'd tried to be nice with me, but I just didn't want to be with her right now. She stared for a minute, deliberately checked her car still had wheels and drove away.

The next day I was slightly late for the meeting, immediately handing Bill the notes from the Marley meeting. Bill grudgingly accepted them. Before any more could be said, June, Bill's secretary came in and said there was an emergency meeting on the pay claim response and everyone available should go to the Personnel Manager's office right away. We all laughed and made our way out and over to the main office. As we left Bill said, 'It feels like a conspiracy against ever holding this bloody clocking policy meeting,' walking out in a huff. I studiously avoided Anita as we walked up to the main offices.

— **24** —

Suicide

That evening at around 8 p.m. the phone rang. I struggled up from the sofa stiff and cold to answer it.

'Frank it's Bill.'

'Hi. What is it?' I replied.

'My pager's gone off, I'm in the Royal Exchange Theatre in Manchester. It looks like someone's hanged themselves in the press shop basement on evening shift and Jim isn't answering the phone.'

'Shit,' I said. 'What am I supposed to do?'

'I'm not sure, it's never happened before. The superintendent said he's had security call the police and they're there, but are waiting for forensics and have been told to touch nothing. You may need to get personnel files, I'm not sure. Maybe interview people; I don't know. I'll try and get Tim or Anita in as well. I won't be home till midnight though if you need to brief me before the morning.'

'Ok, I'll be there in 15 minutes,' I said.

I drove, brooding all the way over what I could do that might be helpful in the circumstances. When I arrived, I rang the superintendent to get a name so I could take the man's personnel file over, which would have next of kin, home address and so on. When I got to the press shop it was silent, I presumed because the scrap metal dropped into the basement and that's where the body was. The operators were in their tea areas, with a single policeman standing by the entrance stairs to the basement.

'Frank Thomas, I'm covering for the press shop personnel officer, is the superintendent in there?'

'Yes, they're on the right waiting to be interviewed. We're still awaiting forensics. Don't go to the left when you get in.'

'Thanks,' and I walked in. I held my breath then glanced left and dimly saw a body hanging from an RSJ, parts boxes scattered around, blue nylon rope.

'Can't we even cut him down, give him some dignity?' I whispered to the superintendent.

He replied firmly, 'No. Don the first aider and the policeman have checked there's no pulse, we've been firmly told to touch nothing and wait for the police forensics people.'

I looked away, I'd only ever seen a motorcycle accident body before and felt queasy.

The superintendent was holding a note.

'He left this on the table over there,' and handed me the spidery writing on a piece of letterhead, I moved nearer to the ceiling light to read it.

Dear Susan,

I've done this at work so the kids wouldn't find me at home after school. You will be better off without me, rest assured I loved you all. Please say sorry to whoever was unlucky enough to find me.

Bill Whishaw.

'Phew' I said. I sat down at the table, with my back to the body. My hands were shaking as I opened the personnel file and saw two daughters were listed and his age was thirty-eight.

'Does his wife know?' I asked.

'No. The copper on the door said they'll go round to the family as soon as forensics confirms what has happened. The lad that found him is upstairs with the first aider comforting him; he can't go till he's been interviewed. It must have been an hour since he was found, so the forensics are taking their time.'

I sat back, the initial adrenalin was wearing off and I felt tired. I couldn't get the fact that the man had two kids out of my mind; why would they be better off without him? Did he beat them up, was he an addict or something? How could that be? The body was hanging far enough away to be just a shadow, it was like a scene from one of those Western lynching movies.

There was a knock on the door.

'At last,' said the policeman, walking over to the door but it was Anita who walked in, and staggered slightly; the policeman grabbed her arm to steady her. I tried to get up, but my legs had turned to jelly; he brought her over and sat her down next to me at the table. She stared ahead, with a shaking hand I gave her the note to read.

'Children?'

'Yes, two,' I said quietly.

There was a clanging on the stairs as a man and woman in Tyvek-type boilersuits with cameras came into the basement. An inspector followed them in, looked around and said, 'Our apologies for the delay, we were involved in another call. If you could all leave the room please, find an interviewing room upstairs and I'll want to see whoever found the body and some of his closest workmates in about fifteen minutes.' He looked at me, 'Does that file tell me his name, address and so on?'

I replied 'Yes' and handed it to him, along with the handwritten note.

Anita looked round and said, 'Why don't we go to the canteen for a cup of tea before the interviews start? It might help with the shock.'

We nodded and set off behind the superintendent, as Anita and I were not sure of the best way there from the basement. We were all silent as we threaded our way through the eerily silent presses. Suddenly, a runner caught up with us and breathlessly said the police wanted to see the janitor who'd found the body and the first aider right away. The superintendent said he'd go back; I said we'd only be ten minutes and carried on to the canteen with Anita.

It was harshly lit compared with the dingy basement, and busy as none of the press shop operators were working. People turned to stare but no one approached us.

We sat down with our tea; the canteen lady had said it was 'on her.' News travelled fast.

'I can't get over abandoning two children like that however upset he was, it seems so selfish,' I said quietly.

Anita looked over her teacup. 'Frank, you can't say that or even think it, he must have been in extreme pain, clinically depressed…'

'But to put his own feelings before his children?'

Anita stared at me again. I stopped talking.

'Have you ever been depressed Frank?'

'No, I bloody haven't,' I said.

'Well, I have,' and glared at me across the table. 'You know, you can be such an insensitive ass sometimes.'

I looked down, hurt by the comment. Anita continued steadily, 'I'll tell you how it feels some time, the despair, the loneliness, when I tell you about my brother.'

'Yeah, you kept mentioning your brother the night you were half-cut,' I said.

'I thought you said I never said anything?' narrowing her eyes.

'You didn't, you used his name a lot but never said why…'

'It's time to get back I think; they'll be waiting for us,' she said, getting up from the table.

I followed, I could sense the change in atmosphere but had no real idea why and was too tired to think about it now.

'We should let Johnnie Murphy deal with the family, he's better than us at that.' I got the impression she really meant better than me.

When we got back the body had been taken down, the presses were being prepped to roll, and the police inspector was interviewing the man's work colleagues.

He came over to us.

'Thanks for the file, I'll be going round to the family now. We think it's a straightforward "while the balance of his mind was disturbed." My colleague will see a couple more staff but none we have seen so far saw it coming or had any inkling of personal problems. The note he left was short on detail as well.'

We went to see the superintendent. There was nothing else to be done that evening and we decided to go home and meet the next day. I was too tired and overwhelmed to worry about whether I'd upset Anita and we said our goodbyes and walked to the car park.

I thought about my father's generation. They had fought Hitler so people could live their own lives as they wished. How many men did he see drown as a nineteen-year-old while this guy just throws it away in the prime of life? Maybe I shouldn't have said that to Anita, but it still seemed incredibly selfish. What did I know?

The next day, I briefed Jim as he was the press shop PO. I later saw Jim and Johnnie arranging follow up counselling from the industrial chaplain for work colleagues. The incident was closed formally but the shock of it remained throughout the factory. It was there in the air unspoken in every tearoom. In the fifteen years the factory had been open, nothing like it had ever happened before. Bill was writing an internal memo to staff and for the press and Johnnie was planning follow up family visits. Little did we know that there would soon be another tragedy.

25

Crash

A month later, Anita was on holiday visiting relatives overseas with her parents. I had decided over the weekend that I should have one last shot at tying up the many loose ends with her. Some were work related, like I'd never properly spoken to her about the tribunal settlement and the racist foreman. I also wanted to go over the canteen discussion on the suicide. I was still hurt by her comment about me being an insensitive ass, probably because it might be true. I secretly wanted to hear more on what had happened months ago with the supposed fiancé. But whatever, we had not rekindled our relationship anyway. Also nagging me was her brother; every time we stumbled around what had happened to him, she got upset. I recognised that however hard I tried to ignore Anita rationally, I always struggled to. I was resolved not to be at a complete loss as to why our relationship had never got going.

On the Wednesday, Bill popped into my office and carefully shut the door behind him, an ominous sign.

'You may not know yet but the trainee robotics engineer that had the bad car accident has just died.'

'I'm sorry to hear that, the one in Anita's area?' I queried, instantly regretting my choice of words. It was only the second death while driving on company business in ten years so hardly an everyday occurrence. On top of the suicide, it was also the second employee death in a matter of months.

'Yes. Welfare has done all the follow up but there's a delicate matter that has arisen that won't wait for Anita's return.'

'A delicate matter?'

'The industrial chaplain will explain, here's his diocesan number,' handing over a scrap of paper. Keep me up to date, but you're handling this, ok?'

'Handling what?' I persisted.

'It's called delegation. You know what you are doing these days, so listen to the chaplain but do what you think is best. Don't bother me with the detail, I've got too much on with the new model business case,' and then Bill opened the door and left.

I was intrigued; I'd had a few dealings with Canon Brian May the Industrial Chaplain who had a pastoral role. It all seemed a bit nineteenth century to me, but he had good interpersonal skills and was much appreciated by both the operators and the stewards. He always did death in service visits and did talks on alcoholism, drugs and divorce. Like the site occupational medic, he was independent and not short on making a lobbying case for things he didn't agree with.

Brian May breezed into my office on time the next day with his dog collar on.

'The young engineer who died tragically in the car accident was living with another man.'

I replied, 'Yes, a fellow engineer, someone said.'

'Well, they had recently purchased their property together with a joint mortgage,' continued the Canon.

'Like brothers and sisters sometimes do,' I said, not knowing where this was going.

'Quite. Having now spoken to the other boy, they were apparently in a homosexual relationship.'

'Right,' I said puzzled.

'A condition of the mortgage was that they both had life insurance.'

'So, the other lad gets the mortgage paid off then?' I interrupted.

'Yes,' said the Canon, 'but he's told me that the parents didn't know that they are, were, homosexual. Additionally,

228

I noticed at personnel records that he'd recently changed his pension form nominated beneficiary from his parents to the other boy.'

'Ok, so he gets four times salary death in service then as well. Lucky lad in one sense,' I said raising my eyebrows.

'It could be seven times salary; apparently he was driving to a meeting with an engineer at another site when the crash happened, so he was travelling on company business,' continued the Canon. 'Now, that's why I'm here. The pension fund trustees, they can "take into account the member's wishes" but they don't have to. So, if someone were leaving their pension to Battersea Dog's Home and had two kids, they would overrule it.'

'Ok' I said, still puzzled.

'You can make a recommendation to the trustees, but I can't.'

I thought again. 'Ok. ok. Let's see if I've understood you here. You would like the four or even seven times lump sum to go to someone else, is that it?' I said.

'Yes. The parents brought him up, subsidised him through college and don't even know he's homosexual,' the Canon said. 'The boy will get the house and given the length of their relationship, that should be enough.'

I was quiet for a minute, thinking, then said, 'So, he's not "come out" as they say?'

'Apparently not, so his partner says.'

I took another swig of water,

'Does the partner know about the pension lump sum at all?'

'From my one talk with him I would say not,' said the Canon.

'Ok, so you propose we should deceive him, and recommend to the trustees they overturn the deceased wishes?'

'Not in those words but overturn his view yes.'

'If he'd been married to a woman, what would you have recommended?'

'Clearly all to go to the wife. However, I'm sure that if he'd been living in sin with a female partner for only four months, I'd recommend the same action on the pension.'

'Living in sin – common law partner is the correct phrase these days,' I said. The Canon nodded.

'Ok. Whose job is it to tell the parents he was homosexual, first of all then?' I said.

'I'm certainly not and the other boy himself may not either – out of respect to their feelings. He hasn't met the parents yet and won't do till the funeral.'

'When do we need a decision by?' I asked.

'Tomorrow, as the funeral is next Monday and we should tell his parents before then.'

'Ok, I'll get a few views from colleagues and give you a ring tomorrow.'

I took the papers and disappeared to find a conference room where I wouldn't be disturbed to think through what I had heard. It was like moral philosophy at college.

I wrote the Canon's opinion down as a statement and then put the positive and negative arguments in columns underneath. I made the assumption that the pension wishes form would not be legally disclosable but clearly overturning someone's express wishes was a serious matter none the less. I distilled the main arguments down to the shortness of time they had been living together. If they had been heterosexual and married the decision would have been clear. I was concerned about the influence that homosexuality might have on a Church Canon's view of the relationship, as well as the other lad having already got the house paid for through the mortgage life insurance.

I popped back downstairs and found Tim in his office and went through the main arguments with him. I wasn't surprised that he, as a public school educated colonialist, supported the Canon's view, unless there was some evidence that the deceased hated his parents.

Jim, on the other hand, had a simple but surprisingly thoughtful view that was the complete opposite. If the form said the other boy was the beneficiary that is what we should follow. 'Personnel do not play God, whatever the vicar might think,' was Jim's parting comment.

I thought about getting a view from Bill, but he'd made his view clear that I needed to sort it so I would. I rang the Canon, as he needed to talk to the parents and the other lad soon.

'The parents were really proud of him, he got a first from Imperial, London. They sounded on the elderly side but appeared to be close to him. The other news is that the lad has put up a separate bed in the spare room and decided not to tell the parents about the relationship. He said they'd agreed a few weeks ago it was still too soon to tell them and he wanted to respect his late partner's wishes.'

'That's thoughtful of him,' I mused. I took the decision I'd been edging towards; I had agonised over it last night.

'Ok, I'll ring the trustees tomorrow and give them the reasons for overturning his pension form nomination,' I said.

'Good man,' said the Canon.

'Yeah well, I'm just trying to be fair and equitable in this situation, I'm not playing God you know. Four months in a relationship is too short a time for someone to get such huge compensation, hetero or homosexual.'

I wrote up a précis of my reasoning for the pension trustees and gave it to June for typing, with a copy for Bill. I felt satisfied that I had done my best for the whole family in an incredibly tragic and difficult circumstance. It seemed fair that the other lad would get a house paid for through the mortgage insurance, but that the parents would get the death in service compensation. For once, this was an unusually odd feeling of job satisfaction.

26

Anita

I had to go over to the PTA Plant for a meeting on the Red Lion incident. I always enjoyed going there, bright and airy with no welding flashes or presses and jigs crashing around. It was just lots of operators clambering in cars, screwing in lights, putting in windscreens, gluing on badges. It was less physical than, say, spot welding and less dirty, in a nicer environment with lovely solvent and glue smells. Pretty boring in the long run still, I thought.

I got to the personnel offices there to find an operations room, not unlike the original Adelphi Hotel, in full swing. I was gestured to sit down and nodded to the personnel people I'd met on the day of the Red Lion sting. The London lawyer who would represent the company in the tribunal was in full flight on a speaker phone. At the end, they asked me if I had any questions.

'From a process perspective, I'm the picture taker in the pub and will see you tomorrow. I'm just wondering what the point is of Anita coming along as well, as she was just my lunchtime date in the Red Lion?'

The London lawyer had a dramatic type of voice, emphasizing every syllable like Ian Paisley.

'Frank, have you been to a tribunal before?' he asked

'Only as an observer,' I replied.

'Are you worried at all about appearing?'

'Not at all, I'm looking forward to the experience.'

'You should be worried! The union has employed a top notch QC. He's definitely no pussy and very, very clever.'

'I did enough student politics to hold my own in any argument,' I replied, slightly affronted.

'Good man. Now, are you implying this Anita is flaky, because if they think that, they will undoubtedly subpoena her so they can cross-examine her,' he said.

'I'm not no. Why not just say I'm the picture taker and I'm appearing?' I said.

'I'm happy to try that, I'll submit just your name but be in no doubt if they come back and say there were two people she must appear. Ok?'

'Yes, that's fine. I'll be on my own tomorrow,' I said, relieved.

I declined the curled-up sandwiches and walked back to the body plant canteen for lunch. The subassembly areas had finished for lunch, but the lines were all running, for once. I laughed at the monkey gestures and whistles as I walked through the van framing area, where we had disciplined the porn show nightshift.

Tim and Anita were at a Formica canteen table, Anita sheepishly eating cheese and onion pie. I tried hard to stop myself grinning but was not entirely successful.

'Can I join you?' I said as I sat down.

Tim said he had a sickness interview in twenty and had better go and look at the papers, so I found myself opposite Anita.

'Don't look at me like that,' she said trying to look stern.

'Like what?'

'Supercilious holier than thou look,' she smiled through clenched lips.

I remained straight faced,

'Chips as well? Have you been out drinking with that girl from college again?'

'I'm hungry today, I can't think why,' she said in a serious voice. 'My head has felt better.'

'Good. Do you want some good news?' I asked. She looked at me with one eyebrow raised.

'You're not needed tomorrow, and hopefully not at the tribunal either.'

'How's that then?' She continued eating.

'I explained to the barrister that I took the pictures and we couldn't afford to lose both of us for a tribunal that's listed for a week.'

'That's the reason you gave. Ok. Did I say anything that night in the pub when I'd had a few too many?' she asked slowly, all the time looking at my face.

'God, no' I said, trying to sound convincing.

'Really? That's not how I remember it.' She looked at me aggressively.

'It's up to me to take a decision on appearing as a witness like that, not anyone else. I need to cope with my demons, not you.' I looked away, I wondered why I had bothered to think of a reason to keep her away from something she was clearly upset by. I shrugged, put my work personality back on and simply changed the topic as if she'd said nothing.

'I see the pay claim's finally in.'

'Is it?' she said coldly.

'Do you want to know the details?' trying to sound enthusiastic.

'Not really, I'm leaving,' she replied, completely deadpan.

'Oh, are you?' I said.

'So, you didn't know then?'

'No.'

Anita stood,

'Don't take up poker, Frank.' She picked up her tray and walked off. I watched her go, flabbergasted by how it had turned out. There weren't many women in the factory, and I noticed others watch her too, for different reasons. She suddenly stopped, turned back and stared at me; I stared back, pissed off.

'Sod it,' I said to myself, finished the pie and left.

I spent the whole of the next day getting to and from London on British Rail. All for a thirty-minute meeting with the barrister, a waste of time. I wasn't expected to deny being asked by the company to be at the pub at the given time and take some photos; what else was there?

I was looking forward to seeing Pete in the Empire in town that evening, the political situation was deteriorating rapidly. I had read five newspapers and knew we would have a bloody good argument, which always cheered me up.

'Your phoney war, it's over Frank,' was Pete's opening greeting. We bought a couple of pints of Greenall's Bitter and sat down.

'How so?'

'Our research department is saying British Steel is looking to sack 50,000 staff this week and Michael Edwardes at Leyland is shutting two Coventry car plants with 25,000 jobs. With nearly 2 million unemployed you're going see riots man.'

I soon got into it. 'British Leyland has had a billion pounds for new models since 1975, look at them. Absolute crap. People are buying foreign cars because they're better, it's that simple.'

'I thought Michael Edwards was your Tory hero.' Pete exclaimed.

'He's trying to get a grip and give BL a future, but after all these years it's time to pull the plug, say enough is enough. Open your eyes Pete, the Marina, the Princess, the Allegro, what a waste of taxpayers' money.' We argued in circles for half an hour until we ran out of energy, but after travelling all day I decided I wouldn't go for a meal and went home for an early night.

As I mooched back to the car, I was cheered up by people having a good time, the sounds of laughter and the clinking of glasses. I could be vicariously happy for others without feeling left out, it's the way I'd always been. I admitted to myself I was sad about Anita, but what the hell could I do?

The following weeks in work were manic. I saw Anita in the distance sometimes but we were hardly ever in our offices. I'd expected to hear about her job move formally but nothing happened. It was there in my subconscious, but I tried hard to compartmentalise my life and one compartment was Anita, best avoided.

A week later I saw the company reply to the pay claim. I was fascinated to read the official reply to the controversial £242 million profit. It was that half of the profit came from importing models from Europe, as British factories were not producing the cars they should with the people they had. A stunning riposte to the backward unions..

I could see the country deteriorating slowly, it felt like it was moving back to last year, even if officially 'the winter of discontent' was over. But I could also see from that week's *Sun*, that moderate numbers of trade unionists were emerging and distancing themselves from the militants and even crossing picket lines. This was new. The engineering strike was now affecting not just the manufacturing sector but also retail. Shopping centres were closing, having no air con or working lifts. Nothing much seemed to change in Liverpool though; the BL plant had already shut down in Speke and with it 3000 jobs. It now looked like the Pressed Steel no 1 plant was shutting with 1200 jobs at risk. The war of words between government and the unions was getting worse. The TR7 sports car built in Speke was a byword for poor design and poor quality and they couldn't give them away in the USA. Yet Moss Evans, the T and G Union head was threatening 'bloody revolution' if the plant closed. Having been in the job for nearly a year, I knew the unions were total dicks about the precarious future of manufacturing in Britain.

— 27 —

End

I went into work, resolved to invite Anita out one last time. My excuse would be briefing her on work things, but I hoped I would be able to get behind our going nowhere relationship issues. But before I could say anything, she came into my office, shutting the door and announced.

'Hi, I wanted you to be the first to know,' she said,

'I've been offered and have accepted this time, a job at Head Office as senior PO for succession planning.'

'Really?' I croaked. 'Congratulations then,' I continued, 'When do you start?' It was all I could think to say among the conflicting feelings circling inside my head.

'First of next month' said Anita, 'I need a flat in London first.'

'Wow, that's quick.' I was disappointed to realise the discussions had been going on for a while since she'd turned down the training job offer months ago. Maybe that's why things had cooled between us. As if she could read my thoughts, she said, 'I'm not leaving because of you, you know. I've done my penance here and I'm looking for something else.'

That word had given me a way out of the difficult feelings forming.

'Penance?'

'You know I've never been comfortable here, it's always been hard work being a woman in a factory environment.'

'Yes.' I had to agree with her on that.

'Anyway, I definitely want you at my leaving do, so I've come to arrange diaries so you can be there.' She suggested dates, I agreed to one and ostentatiously wrote it in green ink.

I needed to get away, before my feelings overwhelmed me.

'Right, I've got a meeting with a steward. Got to go, see you later,' I said, standing.

'I'm telling everyone else at one o'clock in the canteen, can you be there? She said.

'Sure, I'll do my best.' I moved out, edging past the still sitting Anita, who was looking up at my face. I smiled and collected my clipboard and papers, striding out into the corridor. I bumped into Bill almost immediately.

'You look like you've seen a ghost.' He held my arm.

'I've just heard Anita's news, I suppose I'm a bit upset. Would you mind if I took the rest of the day as holiday?'

Bill looked at me, released my arm and said, 'Forget taking it as holiday, with the suicide and the car crash you've had a tough time recently. I'll see you tomorrow at nine, ok?'

'Thanks,' I said. I waited till Anita had left my office, locked the door and drove home.

I knew I was being irrational, but I was struggling with it all. Ok, I had planned to ask her out one evening again. But we had been out before and things had gone awry, surely the same would have happened this time? Surely?

I was tempted to stop at the Black Bull in Gateacre, but knew I was discombobulated. If I had one to relax, it might go further, so I just drove over the road and down towards the river. I parked and walked past Speke Hall down to the Mersey River. It was cold and drizzly, with some strange ship offloading equipment in the river in front. The airport runway just to the left had a plane coming in to land and, on the other side of the river, the shipyards and oil terminal blinked their lights. I liked the physical space, the sky, the perspective.

I tried to think rationally; she was doing the right thing as she hated the factory and she was ambitious. It was only ever a tick on her CV. It was right for her, I did really wish her every success. She'd worked hard and been there longer than I had. A noisy three engine jet landed, and I looked across. Where had the passengers been, was it business, holiday, visiting relatives? Whatever… it must be better than ten hours a day in a car factory.

Anita leaving had crystallised something in my subconscious. I had really had just about enough of this country, the factory, the job, even Anita. My whole life seemed to be going nowhere. It wasn't what I thought it could be, nothing seemed to be moving forward however hard I tried, and I had tried hard.

I gazed over the river for a little while feeling down. After a while I snapped out of it and resolved to see Bill the next day to resign. Having nearly sacked me twice Bill would probably be pleased. I knew now I didn't want to be an academic, and it didn't look like personnel was a career for me either. I would have to go away and find myself, like those sixties' hippies in California. I had no ties, few financial obligations and no emotional commitments now. I had always been decisive I said to myself without irony. It was done.

I had an untroubled night, I had decided what to do and would do it. I was waiting for Bill when he got in.

'Bill, I just want to say after much careful thought, I've decided to resign forthwith. I know it's a bit out of the blue but here's my letter and I'm happy to work the rest of the month as notice.'

'You're kidding me, right?' said Bill. He sat down and stroked his moustache. 'Look, you can't, we've just had some good news. I can't say any more, but you're part of the plans, so we need you to stay.'

'Really? Well given the number of times I've nearly been sacked, I'm flattered. Maybe it's some good news for the factory but whatever, my mind is made up,' I said. I was shocked, I had never had anyone tell me they wanted me to stay before. It must be Anita leaving and they were short-handed I thought.

'Just hold your horses, this is about Anita moving on isn't it? She said you never showed up for lunch yesterday.'

'Honestly, yes and no. I admire her for thinking about her future and having the courage to try and make it happen. Her move's been the catalyst for me thinking about the future, that's all.'

Bill shoved the letter back across the desk.

'I'm not accepting it right now, take a few days to think it through,' he said.

'We are not an item, Bill whatever you might think,' I said, leaving the letter on the desk as I left.

When I got into my office, Anita looked through the partition and signalled coffee. I shook my head, but she walked round and came in anyway.

'What happened to you at lunchtime yesterday?' she enquired.

'I had to go home, sorry, something came up,' I lied.

She looked intently at me,

'You will be coming to my leaving do, won't you?'

'You know, probably not,' I said. Anita said nothing, held my stare for a while turned slowly round and left.

I worked through the rest of the day in a daze, trying to avoid contact with anyone who might be full of Anita's news. At four o'clock I left and drove home, I wasn't sure I could stand the time before Anita left, I'd lost my appetite for the job.

That night I got home and sat in the car outside the flat. If Bill was implying the news was that the new model was coming to Liverpool, that was fantastic for the families of the workers. I knew in my heart that most of them struggled on with the repetitive jobs so their children had a chance of a better life. I shrugged; if it was the case about the new model, I just didn't get it, as the Tory government had had no impact on the union's behaviour at all. Maybe it was the weaker pound making Britain a cheaper place to invest. I was getting cold so took an A4 pad out of the car and walked to the pub. I sat in a quiet corner and looked at 'Anita's seat,' as if it could change the future.

I tried to be clear about the pluses and minuses of staying, writing on the pad to keep track. My mind went round and round. I knew some of the managers hated me for challenging them, and I knew some of the stewards hated me because of my criticism of the unions. I had a second pint musing on things but went home with nothing resolved.

The next day, I arrived at work to find a summons to Eric's office first thing. I had no real inkling about what the meeting was for but given Bill's reluctance to accept the resignation I wondered if it was related. I hadn't made a major cockup recently, surely? So, what now, even if I had?

Eric sat there, filling his pipe, relaxed and professional looking in his cavernous office. A pot of coffee for two was on the desk in a silver pot with china cups.

'Frank, I want a chat about your future,' he said as he poured.

'Umm, it's a bit late as I've just handed in my resignation,' I said.

'Yes, I heard. There have been some developments though. Two things, in the very strictest confidence,' he said looking up. 'Firstly, the US and Europe have committed the new model here despite our industrial relations difficulty, which is somewhat surprising but welcome news.' He paused to allow that to sink in. 'Secondly, Bill has been appointed personnel manager of the factory in Wales and I want you to stay as an experienced personnel officer here working for his replacement. You're too young for the job at this stage but there could be promotion later if we reorganise.'

I spluttered into the coffee.

'Me? Are you serious?'

'The new model requires a huge investment in robotics, many traditional body plant jobs will be redundant. It will be like that Fiat advert you see on TV for their Strada car, with orange robots doing welding and framing. That's why I've informally suspended the welt working crackdown as many jobs will simply cease to exist. I need someone in the body plant committed to handling a difficult situation, someone who won't bodge a series of short-term fixes and still retains the respect of the unions. I believe you've shown you can do that.' He paused again.

'I also want someone who stands up to production management, who shows personnel can be more than pay, rations and firefighting.'

I had another gulp of the coffee. I didn't know if I was more flabbergasted by the new model coming to the factory, Bill being promoted elsewhere or being asked to stay.

'I'm, I'm honestly flattered to hear all that, I'm really shocked though. If you don't mind, I need to take a few days to think about it. I've just decided to leave as I can't see where I'm making a difference here. I can't see how the unions would stand for me anyway.'

Eric grinned wryly, 'I've made a few enquiries, you seem to have earned their grudging respect after a ropey start.'

We chatted around the state of the country and the industry to finish the coffee and then I left. That evening I mulled over what Eric had said. Bill being promoted was well-deserved, we'd had our differences but there would never be a better personnel manager. I chuckled to myself at the number of times Bill had supported me from being transferred out of labour relations. But why was the company asking me to consider staying, and even a future step up; surely there must be candidates from London or Wales more senior and a lot more experienced? Maybe it was such a thankless job no one in their right mind would be prepared to do it. Although I had made up my mind to leave, I thought of Einstein saying when the facts change, change your mind or something to that effect. Had they changed for me? If so, was I brave enough to change my mind? It might be exciting to help get robotics in, increase productivity and do it without screwing over the staff – a new model for industrial relations? Yeah, Anita was probably right, I was an idealist.

I had a sleepless night. Why hadn't anyone said they had appreciated my efforts before and why did this all happen when I was psychologically committed to leaving? I had always shaped my own life; for better or worse, I had never felt dependent on others' views before.

The rest of the week went by in a daze. I saw Bill looking at me quizzically from afar once or twice, but I managed to avoid Anita due to the ongoing pressure of work meetings.

That Friday night was Anita's leaving do at the Childe of Hale. No one asked if I was going but everyone presumed I would be. I had given very generously to her leaving present and people knew we were often as thick as thieves. I tossed and turned on Thursday night thinking about it and decided that I would go and would wish her all the best but that I wouldn't stay after the speeches were made. I could slope off respectfully after Anita's reply to Bill's valedictory remarks I reasoned.

I drove in silence to the pub, not even listening to my favourite five o'clock news. I was in a bubble, the leaden grey skies of northwest England in the winter oppressed me physically. I arrived at the pub and exchanged small talk in a fug but wasn't really listening. No announcement that Bill was being promoted elsewhere had happened either, which confused me. Bill's speech about Anita was funny and I even smiled when the photos of the Red Lion incident were mentioned. Anita had to stand on a chair to respond, as there were at least twenty-five people there – she was quite the popular girl. I thought she was looking at me sometimes but dismissed it as being like sitting in the front row in a theatre where you feel the actors are looking directly at you but they're not.

After the clapping had died down, I edged outside. I felt an overwhelming relief as my face met the drizzle. I stood getting deliberately wet for a while and then got into my old car. I breathed out and started her up. I had decided I would drive to my flat, park the car and get well and truly at the Black Bull.

I jumped as someone knocked on the passenger window, I couldn't see who through the condensation. The door opened and a dripping wet Anita stood there.

'You were going without saying goodbye?'

I looked over, taken aback.

'I was. I'm sorry, just not up for parting remarks today.'

She got in and sat down, wet. She smoothed her short hair behind one ear looked at me and said, 'Will you drive me home please?'

'What' I said, turning to stare at her car right in front of mine in the car park.

'Will you drive me home and stay the night?' she said again, softly putting her hand on my knee. I jumped.

'But... but it's your leaving do, they'll all miss you.'

'The speeches are over I'll tell Bill I'm leaving and not to worry,' she replied.

She looked past me out of the window,

'Wow, have you seen that?' I turned round and looked over my shoulder, Anita leaned over switched off the ignition and took the keys out.

'Just in case you change your mind,' she smiled. 'I'll get my coat,' getting out of the car.

I was incredulous, had she actually just taken my car keys to stop me driving off?

A few minutes later Anita emerged with her coat, opened the door and handed me back the car keys.

I looked at her quizzically,

'Change my mind, I don't think you even gave me a chance to reply?'

'Too late now, the past is the past. The future never arrives. Can we go?' I shook my head and drove out onto the road to Speke towards Anita's flat. The streetlights glowed, I occasionally glanced left at Anita, still staring straight ahead with her hands on her lap, smiling.

Maybe I should stay in the company, accept the job being offered and see if Anita wanted a weekend relationship travelling between London and Liverpool. I could ask her tonight. That would definitely require a car that started.

Alan Dixon 2020 copyright.

CPSIA information can be obtained
at www.ICGtesting.com
Printed in the USA
LVHW110821120821
694436LV00001B/2